AMERICAN POETS PROJECT

AMERICAN POETS PROJECT

IS PUBLISHED WITH A GIFT IN MEMORY OF

James Merrill

AND SUPPORT FROM ITS FOUNDING PATRONS

Sidney J. Weinberg, Jr. Foundation

The Berkley Foundation

Richard B. Fisher and Jeanne Donovan Fisher

William Carlos Williams

selected poems

robert pinsky editor

AMERICAN POETS PROJECT

THE LIBRARY OF AMERICA

Poems published by permission of New Directions Publishing Corp. See page
178 for copyright information.

The paper used in this publication meets the minimum requirements of the
American National Standard for Information Sciences—Permanence of Paper
for Printed Library Materials, ANSI Z39.48—1984.

Design by Chip Kidd and Mark Melnick.
Frontispiece: Yale Collection of American Literature, Beinecke Rare Book and
Manuscript Library

Library of Congress Cataloging-in-Publication Data:
Williams, William Carlos, 1883–1963.
    [Poems. Selections]
    Selected poems / William Carlos Williams ; Robert Pinsky, editor.
        p. cm. — (American poets project   ;   13)
    Includes bibliographical references and index.
    ISBN 1-931082-71-5 (alk. paper)
     I. Pinsky, Robert. II. Title. III. Series.

PS3545.I544A6 2004
811'.52 — dc22
2004048523

10 9 8 7 6 5 4 3 2 1

William
Carlos
Williams

CONTENTS

INTRODUCTION

In 1917, a 34-year-old medical doctor published a book called *Al Que Quiere!* The title in Spanish (a language he heard in his parents' home) means "to who wants it" or "to him who wants it." The author, who had paid the publisher fifty dollars to cover printing costs, composed the following statement that appears on the dust jacket, in flamboyant typography:

> To Whom It May Concern! This book is a collection of poems by William Carlos Williams. You, gentle reader, will probably not like it, because it is brutally powerful and scornfully crude. Fortunately, neither the author nor the publisher care much whether you like it or not. The author has done his work, and if you *do* read the book, you will agree that he doesn't give a damn for your opinion. . . . And we, the publishers, don't much care whether you buy the book or not. It only costs a dollar, so that we can't make much profit out of it. But we have the satisfaction of offering that which will outweigh, in spite of its eighty small

pages, a dozen volumes of pretty lyrics. We have the profound satisfaction of publishing a book in which, we venture to predict, the poets of the future will dig for material as the poets of today dig in Whitman's *Leaves of Grass*.

Part anti-blurb, part manifesto; part plain American vernacular ("it only costs a dollar") and part paradoxical avant-garde ("you will agree that he doesn't give a damn"); eager for attention under the transparent disdain, yet genuinely insouciant as well—the most remarkable thing about this little statement, which parodies both American commercialism and European aestheticism while embracing them, is that the concluding sentence turns out to be quite true. Generations of poets have indeed dug into the poems of *Al Que Quiere!* and the other works of William Carlos Williams.

Young poets still admire the enduring freshness, for example, of "Danse Russe" from *Al Que Quiere!*, which in a way fulfills the dust jacket's promise to be "scornfully crude," and in a way complicates or denies that phrase by being subtle rather than simply crude, and engaging rather than scornful:

> If I when my wife is sleeping
> and the baby and Kathleen
> are sleeping
> and the sun is a flame-white disc
> in silken mists
> above shining trees,—
> if I in my north room
> dance naked, grotesquely
> before my mirror
> waving my shirt round my head
> and singing softly to myself:
> "I am lonely, lonely.
> I was born to be lonely,
> I am best so!"

If I admire my arms, my face,
my shoulders, flanks, buttocks
against the yellow drawn shades,—

Who shall say I am not
the happy genius of my household?

This is plain, yet not plain. If we call the manner of the poem's language "naked" like the dance it describes, we have to recognize that this is a complicated nakedness. If you like the predictable, and prefer easy categories, "You will probably not like it."

From beginning to end—from the title in French (another language spoken in Williams' childhood home) to the slightly formal word "household"—the poem enjoys playing elevation against directness, candor against enigma, the ordinary against the strange.

Clearly, if you expect poetry to use end-rhyme and to expound lofty sentiments in noble terms, as in the nineteenth century, the poem defies your expectations—but on the other hand, "the sun is a flame-white disc / in silken mists" does demonstrate that as a young poet Williams was obsessed with Keats, and in his own words, "I knew *Palgrave's Golden Treasury* by heart."

Clearly, if you expect Williams to concentrate only on visual images, in the most colloquial language, the poem's gleeful putting forth of sensibility and the comedy of personality, its pleasure in the slightly formal names for body parts, its relish for the old sense of the word "genius," its use of "grotesquely" and the choice of "household" rather than "house" or "family" all defy your expectations—but on the other hand, the "yellow drawn shades" and the "shining trees" in that early morning mist are vivid, and a lot of the language, like "waving my shirt round my head" is plain American, plain as can be.

In other words, the nose-thumbing but transparently eager and anxious insouciance of the dust jacket has a deeper, more durable counterpart in the actual poems: reader, try to listen and see freshly, and leave expectations and cliches behind. Notions of purity will find themselves off-balance, and everything is liable to be either a little more familiar, or a little less familiar, than you might think.

Even the poet's name keeps the reader off balance enough to avoid lazy ideas: "To Whom It May Concern! This book is a collection of poems by William Carlos Williams." Early on, he tinkered with this, signing his first book "William C. Williams." After that, he seriously considered using "W. C. Williams," then decided to use the full name: the almost comically ordinary and similar first name and last name on either side escorting the central, exotic "Carlos."

The name among other things is the more American because it is hybrid, implying an immigrant story. Williams said of his father, an English liberal and Unitarian who worked for an international cologne-water company, that he was a European all his life; his Caribbean mother spoke mainly French and German. In some ways, for a young medical man to be interested in experimental writing and visual art, as Williams was, is in the European tradition of the scientist as the progressive, the doctor who argues with the village priest and advocates vaccination and open-minded acceptance of the new.

The hero of Williams' immigrant story was his father's mother, Emily Dickinson Wellcome. He wrote about her repeatedly, as in "The Last Words of My English Grandmother" and also in "Dedication for a Plot of Ground":

> This plot of ground
> facing the waters of this inlet
> is dedicated to the living presence of

Emily Dickinson Wellcome
who was born in England; married;
lost her husband and with
her five year old son
sailed for New York in a two-master;
was driven to the Azores;
ran adrift on Fire Island shoal,
met her second husband
in a Brooklyn boarding house,
went with him to Puerto Rico
bore three more children, lost
her second husband, lived hard
for eight years in St. Thomas,
Puerto Rico, San Domingo, followed
the eldest son to New York,
lost her daughter, lost her "baby,"
seized the two boys of
the oldest son by the second marriage
mothered them—they being
motherless— fought for them
against the other grandmother
and the aunts, brought them here
summer after summer, defended
herself here against thieves,
storms, sun, fire,
against flies, against girls
that came smelling about, against
drought, against weeds, storm-tides,
neighbors, weasels that stole her chickens,
against the weakness of her own hands,
against the growing strength of
the boys, against wind, against
the stones, against trespassers,
against rents, against her own mind.

She grubbed this earth with her own hands,
domineered over this grass plot,

blackguarded her oldest son
into buying it, lived here fifteen years,
attained a final loneliness and—

If you can bring nothing to this place
but your carcass, keep out.

The characteristic American immigration story, with
its accidents and family break-ups, the hard-to-track se-
quence of marriages and half-siblings, the grandmother
raising the boys after fighting the other grandmother for
them—all this suggests Williams' affinity with the immi-
grant Polish, Italian, and Jewish families he treated and
wrote about.

Without the eclectic spirit of the "Carlos," the
"Williams" is not American enough. Even the year
Williams and his brother spent attending school in Swit-
zerland as teenagers seems to be part of his awareness of
an American idiom and American manners, with mixing
and unlikely hybrids near the center. His first two guiding
stars in poetry were Keats and Whitman, and some of the
casual precision, the rangy, raunchy elegance of his writing,
may come from a unique, all-but-impossible melding of
ingredients from those masters—though Williams' vivid-
ness not simply of image, but of sensibility, is unique and
sourceless.

But what about academic categories—isn't William
Carlos Williams an *Imagist*? Doesn't he attach a lot of im-
portance to really good descriptions of wheelbarrows and
such? "No ideas but in things"? Yes, but that phrase from
"A Sort of a Song" presents an idea, as Williams well knew
when he wrote it. And it is comes between two imperative
verbs: "Compose" and "Invent!" His way of seeing images
is social, intellectual, quick of mind as well as eye, as in
"Fine Work with Pitch and Copper":

Now they are resting
in the fleckless light
separately in unison

like the sacks
of sifted stone stacked
regularly by twos

about the flat roof
ready after lunch
to be opened and strewn

The copper in eight
foot strips has been
beaten lengthwise

down the center at right
angles and lies ready
to edge the coping

One still chewing
picks up a copper strip
and runs his eye along it.

This definition by example of how you run your eye along a scene incorporates not only the fairly grand diction of "fleckless" combined with the utter plainness of "flat roof" and "eight / foot strips"—but also the elegance of "strewn" and "coping" which are part of the language of a craft, language that will sound always a little archaic because it is in the nature of crafts to conserve their precisions.

The doctor we can imagine looking from an office window at the roofers on their lunch break, with a piece of paper loaded in his typewriter ready between patient appointments, sees that gesture of the worker's eye enjoying the luxury of sighting down the material, still chewing. The gesture is a model of relaxed, athletically focused attention: an allegory for poetry if we choose it to be, but also a specific moment of life, fresh as the sunlight and solid as the regular sacks of stone. Every thing in the poem glows with the poet's idea of it, as he runs his eye along the scene.

Such seeing, and such fine verbal work, require a livelier attention from the reader than any mere symbol-mongering or shuffling of "isms." Williams' poetry does not invite the kind of literary-critical explication that finds much to do in the work of his great contemporaries such as Wallace Stevens and T. S. Eliot. (Maybe this is one reason why Williams viewed Eliot as his antithesis, and found his ascendancy discouraging.) What is apparent, what is evident—and the infinite richness of what is apparent—is Williams' subject, and the style he developed demands that the reader supply something a little more like alertness than explanation.

For example, the play of consonants and vowels in "Fine Work with Pitch and Copper" should be heard: the chiastic arrangement of sounds in "picks up a copper strip"; the luxuriant play among "resting," "fleckless," and "separately"; the similar play among "twos," "roof," and "strewn"; the way those last two elements are linked by how "coping" and "chewing" pick them up. Such writing demonstrates—once you get end-rhyme out of your head —what a master of rhyme Williams is. That is one of the qualities that distinguishes him from his imitators.

Here in "To a Poor Old Woman" is another example of Williams' attention to surfaces, and their immeasurable subtlety. It is also an example of how he simultaneously honors "thing" and "idea," and of his formal mastery:

> munching a plum on
> the street a paper bag
> of them in her hand
>
> They taste good to her
> They taste good

to her. They taste
good to her

You can see it by
the way she gives herself
to the one half
sucked out in her hand

Comforted
a solace of ripe plums
seeming to fill the air
They taste good to her

The sentence that the poem chooses to analyze, with two
different emphases by enjambment, is a wonderful exam-
ple of how richly complicated the simple perception can
be: what is it you can see? You can see a process, which is
itself a process of perception, with a subjective person as
the process's object; *you* can actually *see* that the *plums* taste
good to *her*: an ordinary and extraordinary complex mo-
ment of observation, a current between subjectivities, that
depends upon your visual and social awareness. If you are
inattentive you may not see it ("you can," or you cannot),
and at an even higher level of attention, you can be aware
that your seeing is no simple matter. A little object lesson
in how manifold the surface is, the almost hectoring repe-
titions of the phrase also provide a lecture on the poetic
line. The line ending presents not necessarily a mechani-
cally recurring pause but a degree of tension and arrival,
with the degree different every time. No two spaces be-
tween words, like no two moments in time, are exactly
alike. You can hear it by how he arranges the lines.

Williams' friend from their university days at Penn,
Ezra Pound, describes poetry as a centaur: mind and body,
both parts mobile, each with its alertness, physical and
intellectual. Williams deserves credit for all sorts of intel-
lectual attention: to history, to daily life, to politics. His

historical retellings, his short stories, and the novel *White Mule* would make him an important American writer if he had never written a poem. His painterly alertness to what he sees is only part of the story.

In keeping with the standard of alertness, Williams is perhaps the first poet to describe the landscape as it looks not as someone walks through it, or sees it from a building, but as it appears from a car. This too is a matter not only of visual but of social attention. In "The Young Housewife," published in 1916, he records the sounds and sights as he passes "solitary in my car" but also notes that one can gesture while at the wheel:

> The noiseless wheels of my car
> rush with a crackling sound over
> dried leaves as I bow and pass smiling.

If we think that poetry is a matter of "the hidden meaning," we will miss the emanations of meaning from such sharp, defining perceptions. The smile and bow at the wheel of the car, like the process of seeing that some plums taste good to someone else, involves discovery, a significant moment of manners and feeling that might have been missed. Mystery and meaning inhere in the ordinary, even in the car. The large, terrifying ending of the poem that begins "The pure products of America / go crazy" lands on the innocuous, American word: "No one / to witness / and adjust, no one to drive the car."

The enormous and inexhaustible achievement of these poems is to penetrate American life, in the hybrid and syncretic, evolving American idiom, without collapsing into something stale and predictable: maintaining the astonishment and speed. Here, for example, is a poem from "The Descent of Winter" that sees the language and imagery of advertising with neither illusion nor easy sarcasm, and rises to wonder.

The moon, the dried weeds
and the Pleiades—

Seven feet tall
the dark, dried weedstalks
make a part of the night
a red lace
on the blue milky sky

Write—
by a small lamp

the Pleiades are almost
nameless
and the moon is tilted
and halfgone

And in runningpants and
with ecstatic, æsthetic faces
on the illumined
signboard are leaping
over printed hurdles and
"1/4 of their energy comes from bread"

two
gigantic highschool boys
ten feet tall

A kind of American landscape poem, this gets its energy
partly from the presence of the poet in the landscape, next
to his lamp, pursuing his art without rejecting the "illu-
mined" signboard, or being overwhelmed by the ad or by
the culture that creates it and him and the "printed hur-
dles." Williams is regarded sometimes as a poet of the eye,
which is just only if the eye is considered a metonymy for
the entire soul. The adult, poised, unexhausted eye that
sees those faces "ecstatic, æsthetic" records them in the
shared landscape that encompasses the weeds, the Pleiades,
the bread slogan in a coherent vision. Linking the Pleiades

and the weeds, the ecstatic and the hurdles, the Sappho allusion and the slogan—linking the different kinds of words along with the realms the words suggest—that is the object of his imperative, "Write."

"Ecstatic, æsthetic"—it's an attribute of poetry as of dreams that every thing can seem to apply to the dreamer, with every figure a self-portrait. So in a couple of late poems, a temptation to find the poet. "Passer Domesticus," about the ordinary sparrow, may be a portrait less of the artist or his work than of his approach to all subjects:

> Shabby little bird
> I suppose it's
> the story every-
> where, if you're
>
> domestic you're drab.
> Peep peep!
> The nightingale
> 's your cousin but
>
> these flagrant
> amours get you no-
>
> where. Dull
> to the eye you have
>
> crept in unmolested.

The eye to which this bird is "dull" has not molested it, and has underestimated it. Williams' music, the all-but-rhyming vowels and consonants interlaced with the super-fast enjambments, is itself quick, active, unobtrusive: "unmolested" chiming with the different sounds of "Dull" and "crept in," for example, or the cadenza in the key of "r" hidden in "I suppose it's / the story every- / where, if you're . . ."

Another possibly self-reflecting image concerns what it means to leave the world, or to be about to leave the world. A 1961 news story about the Russian cosmonaut Yuri Gagarin inspired "Heel & Toe to the End." Williams makes Gagarin's voyage an emblem of the ordinary and the ecstatic, being off the earth and of it, quotidian and elevated, comically inebriated by experience, and making an art of it:

> Gagarin says, in ecstasy,
> he could have
> gone on forever
>
> he floated
> ate and sang
> and when he emerged from that
>
> one hundred eight minutes off
> the surface of
> the earth he was smiling
>
> Then he returned
> to take his place
> among the rest of us
>
> from all that division and
> subtraction a measure
> toe and heel
>
> heel and toe he felt
> as if he had
> been dancing

As ever, there's a toughness to this, a clear-sighted quality that makes the poem something quite different from a cosmetically elevated version of leaving the earth—whether by impending death or by technology. "[H]e floated / ate and sang" is ecstatic, but there's something counter to ecstasy and matter of fact in the notion of division, subtraction, and measure being part of that gravity-free space dance.

Freedom exhilarates Williams—the parts of *Spring and All* mix prose and verse, and are numbered in no particular sequence, mixing Arabic and Roman numerals, with "Chapter 2" coming in the middle, followed by Chapter "XXIX" and "Chapter I," with "Chapter XIII" printed upside down: for the hell of it, or to clown us into noticing that great work doesn't follow obvious rules. The little domestic sparrow and the space-dancing Russian infiltrate conventional defenses from the directions of the ordinary or the charming, but they are also "brutally powerful," and as eager to tease us toward thought as the jacket copy on *Al Que Quiere!* "To him who wants it"—but *querer* is also the verb for "love." The simultaneous scorn and courtship, plainness and magnitude, are part of the point: the evident and the domestic can be brutally powerful. As the closing sentence of "A Sort of Song" says, "Saxifrage is my flower that splits / the rocks."

Robert Pinsky
2004

Peace on Earth

The Archer is wake!
The Swan is flying!
Gold against blue
An Arrow is lying.
There is hunting in heaven—
Sleep safe till tomorrow.

The Bears are abroad!
The Eagle is screaming!
Gold against blue
Their eyes are gleaming!
Sleep!
Sleep safe till tomorrow.

The Sisters lie
With their arms intertwining;
Gold against blue
Their hair is shining!
The Serpent writhes!
Orion is listening!
Gold against blue
His sword is glistening!
Sleep!
There is hunting in heaven—
Sleep safe till tomorrow.

Con Brio

Miserly, is the best description of that poor fool
Who holds Lancelot to have been a morose fellow,
Dolefully brooding over the events which had naturally
    to follow
The high time of his deed with Guinevere.
He has a sick historical sight, if I judge rightly,
To believe any such thing as that ever occurred.
But, by the god of blood, what else is it that has deterred
Us all from an out and out defiance of fear
But this same perdamnable miserliness,
Which cries about our necks how we shall have less
    and less
Than we have now if we spend too wantonly?
Bah, this sort of slither is below contempt!
In the same vein we should have apple trees exempt
From bearing anything but pink blossoms all the year,
Fixed permanent lest their bellies wax unseemly, and
    the dear
Innocent days of them be wasted quite.
How can we have less? Have we not the deed?
Lancelot thought little, spent his gold and rode to fight
Mounted, if God was willing, on a good steed.

Aux Imagistes

I think I have never been so exalted
As I am now by you,
O frost bitten blossoms,
That are unfolding your wings
From out the envious black branches.

Bloom quickly and make much of the sunshine.
The twigs conspire against you!
Hear them!
They hold you from behind!

You shall not take wing
Except wing by wing, brokenly,
And yet—
Even they
Shall not endure for ever.

Metric Figure

Veils of clarity
have succeeded
veils of color
that wove
as the sea
sliding above
submerged whiteness.

Veils of clarity
reveal sand
glistening—
falling away
to an edge—
sliding
beneath the advancing ripples.

Stillness

Heavy white rooves
of Rutherford
sloping west and east
under the fast darkening sky:

What have I to say to you
that you may whisper it to them
in the night?

Round you
is a great smouldering distance
on all sides
that engulfs you
in utter loneliness.

Lean above their beds tonight
snow covered rooves;
listen;
feel them stirring warmly within
and say—nothing.

The Young Housewife

At ten A.M. the young housewife
moves about in negligee behind
the wooden walls of her husband's house.
I pass solitary in my car.

Then again she comes to the curb
to call the ice-man, fish-man, and stands
shy, uncorseted, tucking in
stray ends of hair, and I compare her
to a fallen leaf.

The noiseless wheels of my car
rush with a crackling sound over
dried leaves as I bow and pass smiling.

Pastoral

When I was younger
it was plain to me
I must make something of myself.
Older now
I walk back streets
admiring the houses
of the very poor:
roof out of line with sides
the yards cluttered
with old chicken wire, ashes,

furniture gone wrong;
the fences and outhouses
built of barrel-staves
and parts of boxes, all,
if I am fortunate,
smeared a bluish green
that properly weathered
pleases me best
of all colors.

No one
will believe this
of vast import to the nation.

Metric Figure

There is a bird in the poplars!
It is the sun!
The leaves are little yellow fish
swimming in the river.
The bird skims above them,
day is on his wings.
Phoebus!
It is he that is making
the great gleam among the poplars!
It is his singing
outshines the noise
of leaves clashing in the wind.

Apology

Why do I write today?

The beauty of
the terrible faces
of our nonentities
stirs me to it:

colored women
day workers—
old and experienced—
returning home at dusk
in cast off clothing
faces like
old Florentine oak.

Also

the set pieces
of your faces stir me—
leading citizens—
but not
in the same way.

Pastoral

The little sparrows
hop ingenuously
about the pavement
quarreling
with sharp voices
over those things
that interest them.
But we who are wiser
shut ourselves in
on either hand
and no one knows
whether we think good
or evil.
　　Meanwhile,
the old man who goes about
gathering dog-lime
walks in the gutter
without looking up
and his tread
is more majestic than
that of the Episcopal minister
approaching the pulpit
of a Sunday.
　　These things
astonish me beyond words.

El Hombre

It's a strange courage
you give me ancient star:

Shine alone in the sunrise
toward which you lend no part!

Danse Russe

If I when my wife is sleeping
and the baby and Kathleen
are sleeping
and the sun is a flame-white disc
in silken mists
above shining trees,—
if I in my north room
dance naked, grotesquely
before my mirror
waving my shirt round my head
and singing softly to myself:
"I am lonely, lonely.
I was born to be lonely,
I am best so!"
If I admire my arms, my face,
my shoulders, flanks, buttocks
against the yellow drawn shades,—

Who shall say I am not
the happy genius of my household?

Smell!

Oh strong-ridged and deeply hollowed
nose of mine! what will you not be smelling?
What tactless asses we are, you and I, boney nose,
always indiscriminate, always unashamed,
and now it is the souring flowers of the bedraggled
poplars: a festering pulp on the wet earth
beneath them. With what deep thirst
we quicken our desires
to that rank odor of a passing springtime!
Can you not be decent? Can you not reserve your
      ardors
for something less unlovely? What girl will care
for us, do you think, if we continue in these ways?
Must you taste everything? Must you know everything?
Must you have a part in everything?

Spring Strains

In a tissue-thin monotone of blue-grey buds
crowded erect with desire against
the sky—
            tense blue-grey twigs
slenderly anchoring them down, drawing
them in—

            two blue-grey birds chasing
a third struggle in circles, angles,

swift convergings to a point that bursts
instantly!

       Vibrant bowing limbs
pull downward, sucking in the sky
that bulges from behind, plastering itself
against them in packed rifts, rock blue
and dirty orange!

                            But—
(Hold hard, rigid jointed trees!)
the blinding and red-edged sun-blur—
creeping energy, concentrated
counterforce—welds sky, buds, trees,
rivets them in one puckering hold!
Sticks through! Pulls the whole
counter-pulling mass upward, to the right,
locks even the opaque, not yet defined
ground in a terrific drag that is
loosening the very tap-roots!

On a tissue-thin monotone of blue-grey buds
two blue-grey birds, chasing a third,
at full cry! Now they are
flung outward and up—disappearing suddenly!

January Morning

Suite:

I

I have discovered that most of
the beauties of travel are due to
the strange hours we keep to see them:

the domes of the Church of
the Paulist Fathers in Weehawken
against a smoky dawn—the heart stirred—
are beautiful as Saint Peters
approached after years of anticipation.

II

Though the operation was postponed
I saw the tall probationers
in their tan uniforms
                              hurrying to breakfast!

III

—and from basement entries
neatly coiffed, middle aged gentlemen
with orderly moustaches and
well-brushed coats

IV

—and the sun, dipping into the avenues
streaking the tops of
the irregular red houselets,

and

the gay shadows dropping and dropping.

V

—and a young horse with a green bed-quilt
on his withers shaking his head:
bared teeth and nozzle high in the air!

VI

—and a semicircle of dirt-colored men
about a fire bursting from an old
ash can,

VII

—and the worn,
blue car rails (like the sky!)
gleaming among the cobbles!

VIII

—and the rickety ferry-boat "Arden"!
What an object to be called "Arden"
among the great piers,—on the
ever new river!
"Put me a Touchstone
at the wheel, white gulls, and we'll
follow the ghost of the *Half Moon*
to the North West Passage—and through!
(at Albany!) for all that!"

IX

Exquisite brown waves—long
circlets of silver moving over you!
enough with crumbling ice crusts among you!
The sky has come down to you,
lighter than tiny bubbles, face to
face with you!
His spirit is
a white gull with delicate pink feet
and a snowy breast for you to
hold to your lips delicately!

X

The young doctor is dancing with happiness
in the sparkling wind, alone
at the prow of the ferry! He notices
the curdy barnacles and broken ice crusts
left at the slip's base by the low tide
and thinks of summer and green
shell-crusted ledges among
the emerald eel-grass!

XI

Who knows the Palisades as I do
knows the river breaks east from them
above the city—but they continue south
—under the sky—to bear a crest of
little peering houses that brighten
with dawn behind the moody
water-loving giants of Manhattan.

XII

Long yellow rushes bending
above the white snow patches;
purple and gold ribbon
of the distant wood:
>   what an angle
you make with each other as
you lie there in contemplation.

XIII

Work hard all your young days
and they'll find you too, some morning
staring up under
your chiffonier at its warped
bass-wood bottom and your soul—
out!
—among the little sparrows
behind the shutter.

XIV

—and the flapping flags are at
half mast for the dead admiral.

XV

All this—
>   was for you, old woman.
I wanted to write a poem
that you would understand.
For what good is it to me
if you can't understand it?
>   But you got to try hard—

But—
　　Well, you know how
the young girls run giggling
on Park Avenue after dark
when they ought to be home in bed?
Well,
that's the way it is with me somehow.

To a Solitary Disciple

Rather notice, mon cher,
that the moon is
tilted above
the point of the steeple
than that its color
is shell-pink.

Rather observe
that it is early morning
than that the sky
is smooth
as a turquoise.

Rather grasp
how the dark
converging lines
of the steeple
meet at the pinnacle—
perceive how

its little ornament
tries to stop them—

See how it fails!
See how the converging lines
of the hexagonal spire
escape upward—
receding, dividing!
—sepals
that guard and contain
the flower!

Observe
how motionless
the eaten moon
lies in the protecting lines.

It is true:
in the light colors
of morning
brown-stone and slate
shine orange and dark blue.

But observe
the oppressive weight
of the squat edifice!
Observe
the jasmine lightness
of the moon.

Dedication for a Plot of Ground

This plot of ground
facing the waters of this inlet
is dedicated to the living presence of
Emily Dickinson Wellcome
who was born in England; married;
lost her husband and with
her five year old son
sailed for New York in a two-master;
was driven to the Azores;
ran adrift on Fire Island shoal,
met her second husband
in a Brooklyn boarding house,
went with him to Puerto Rico
bore three more children, lost
her second husband, lived hard
for eight years in St. Thomas,
Puerto Rico, San Domingo, followed
the oldest son to New York,
lost her daughter, lost her "baby,"
seized the two boys of
the oldest son by the second marriage
mothered them—they being
motherless—fought for them
against the other grandmother
and the aunts, brought them here
summer after summer, defended
herself here against thieves,
storms, sun, fire,
against flies, against girls

that came smelling about, against
drought, against weeds, storm-tides,
neighbors, weasels that stole her chickens,
against the weakness of her own hands,
against the growing strength of
the boys, against wind, against
the stones, against trespassers,
against rents, against her own mind.

She grubbed this earth with her own hands,
domineered over this grass plot,
blackguarded her oldest son
into buying it, lived here fifteen years,
attained a final loneliness and—

If you can bring nothing to this place
but your carcass, keep out.

Love Song

I lie here thinking of you:—

the stain of love
is upon the world!
Yellow, yellow, yellow
it eats into the leaves,
smears with saffron
the horned branches that lean
heavily

against a smooth purple sky!
There is no light
only a honey-thick stain
that drips from leaf to leaf
and limb to limb
spoiling the colors
of the whole world—

you far off there under
the wine-red selvage of the west!

Le Médecin Malgré Lui

Oh I suppose I should
wash the walls of my office
polish the rust from
my instruments and keep them
definitely in order
build shelves in the laboratory
empty out the old stains
clean the bottles
and refill them, buy
another lens, put
my journals on edge instead of
letting them lie flat
in heaps—then begin
ten years back and
gradually
read them to date

cataloguing important
articles for ready reference.
I suppose I should
read the new books.
If to this I added
a bill at the tailor's
and at the cleaner's
grew a decent beard
and cultivated a look
of importance—
Who can tell? I might be
a credit to my Lady Happiness
and never think anything
but a white thought!

A Coronal

New books of poetry will be written
New books and unheard of manuscripts
will come wrapped in brown paper
and many and many a time
the postman will bow
and sidle down the leaf-plastered steps
thumbing over other men's business.

But we ran ahead of it all.
One coming after
could have seen her footprints

in the wet and followed us
among the stark chestnuts.

Anemones sprang where she pressed
and cresses
stood green in the slender source—
And new books of poetry
will be written, leather-colored oakleaves
many and many a time.

To Mark Anthony in Heaven

This quiet morning light
reflected, how many times
from grass and trees and clouds
enters my north room
touching the walls with
grass and clouds and trees.
Anthony,
trees and grass and clouds.
Why did you follow
that beloved body
with your ships at Actium?
I hope it was because
you knew her inch by inch
from slanting feet upward
to the roots of her hair
and down again and that
you saw her

above the battle's fury—
clouds and trees and grass—

For then you are
listening in heaven.

Portrait of a Lady

Your thighs are appletrees
whose blossoms touch the sky.
Which sky? The sky
where Watteau hung a lady's
slipper. Your knees
are a southern breeze—or
a gust of snow. Agh! what
sort of man was Fragonard?
—as if that answered
anything. Ah, yes—below
the knees, since the tune
drops that way, it is
one of those white summer days,
the tall grass of your ankles
flickers upon the shore—
Which shore?—
the sand clings to my lips—
Which shore?
Agh, petals maybe. How
should I know?
Which shore? Which shore?
I said petals from an appletree.

Willow Poem

It is a willow when summer is over,
a willow by the river
from which no leaf has fallen nor
bitten by the sun
turned orange or crimson.
The leaves cling and grow paler,
swing and grow paler
over the swirling waters of the river
as if loath to let go,
they are so cool, so drunk with
the swirl of the wind and of the river—
oblivious to winter,
the last to let go and fall
into the water and on the ground.

Approach of Winter

The half-stripped trees
struck by a wind together,
bending all,
the leaves flutter drily
and refuse to let go
or driven like hail
stream bitterly out to one side
and fall
where the salvias, hard carmine,—
like no leaf that ever was—
edge the bare garden.

January

Again I reply to the triple winds
running chromatic fifths of derision
outside my window:
                              Play louder.
You will not succeed. I am
bound more to my sentences
the more you batter at me
to follow you.
                              And the wind,
as before, fingers perfectly
its derisive music.

To Waken an Old Lady

Old age is
a flight of small
cheeping birds
skimming
bare trees
above a snow glaze.
Gaining and failing
they are buffeted
by a dark wind—
But what?
On harsh weedstalks
the flock has rested,
the snow

is covered with broken
seedhusks
and the wind tempered
by a shrill
piping of plenty.

Complaint

They call me and I go.
It is a frozen road
past midnight, a dust
of snow caught
in the rigid wheeltracks.
The door opens.
I smile, enter and
shake off the cold.
Here is a great woman
on her side in the bed.
She is sick,
perhaps vomiting,
perhaps laboring
to give birth to
a tenth child. Joy! Joy!
Night is a room
darkened for lovers,
through the jalousies the sun
has sent one gold needle!
I pick the hair from her eyes
and watch her misery
with compassion.

Thursday

I have had my dream—like others—
and it has come to nothing, so that
I remain now carelessly
with feet planted on the ground
and look up at the sky—
feeling my clothes about me,
the weight of my body in my shoes,
the rim of my hat, air passing in and out
at my nose—and decide to dream no more.

Play

Subtle, clever brain, wiser than I am,
by what devious means do you contrive
to remain idle? Teach me, O master.

Complete Destruction

It was an icy day.
We buried the cat,
then took her box
and set match to it

in the back yard.
Those fleas that escaped
earth and fire
died by the cold.

Queen-Anne's-Lace

Her body is not so white as
anemone petals nor so smooth—nor
so remote a thing. It is a field
of the wild carrot taking
the field by force; the grass
does not raise above it.
Here is no question of whiteness,
white as can be, with a purple mole
at the center of each flower.
Each flower is a hand's span
of her whiteness. Wherever
his hand has lain there is
a tiny purple blemish. Each part
is a blossom under his touch
to which the fibres of her being
stem one by one, each to its end,
until the whole field is a
white desire, empty, a single stem,
a cluster, flower by flower,
a pious wish to whiteness gone over—
or nothing.

Waiting

When I am alone I am happy.
The air is cool. The sky is
flecked and splashed and wound
with color. The crimson phalloi
of the sassafras leaves
hang crowded before me
in shoals on the heavy branches.
When I reach my doorstep
I am greeted by
the happy shrieks of my children
and my heart sinks.
I am crushed.

Are not my children as dear to me
as falling leaves or
must one become stupid
to grow older?
It seems much as if Sorrow
had tripped up my heels.
Let us see, let us see!
What did I plan to say to her
when it should happen to me
as it has happened now?

Arrival

And yet one arrives somehow,
finds himself loosening the hooks of
her dress
in a strange bedroom—
feels the autumn
dropping its silk and linen leaves
about her ankles.
The tawdry veined body emerges
twisted upon itself
like a winter wind . . . !

Blueflags

I stopped the car
to let the children down
where the streets end
in the sun
at the marsh edge
and the reeds begin
and there are small houses
facing the reeds
and the blue mist
in the distance
with grapevine trellises
with grape clusters
small as strawberries
on the vines

and ditches
running springwater
that continue the gutters
with willows over them.
The reeds begin
like water at a shore
their pointed petals waving
dark green and light.
But blueflags are blossoming
in the reeds
which the children pluck
chattering in the reeds
high over their heads
which they part
with bare arms to appear
with fists of flowers
till in the air
there comes the smell
of calamus
from wet, gummy stalks.

The Widow's Lament in Springtime

Sorrow is my own yard
where the new grass
flames as it has flamed
often before but not
with the cold fire
that closes round me this year.

Thirtyfive years
I lived with my husband.
The plumtree is white today
with masses of flowers.
Masses of flowers
load the cherry branches
and color some bushes
yellow and some red
but the grief in my heart
is stronger than they
for though they were my joy
formerly, today I notice them
and turn away forgetting.
Today my son told me
that in the meadows,
at the edge of the heavy woods
in the distance, he saw
trees of white flowers.
I feel that I would like
to go there
and fall into those flowers
and sink into the marsh near them.

The Lonely Street

School is over. It is too hot
to walk at ease. At ease
in light frocks they walk the streets
to while the time away.

They have grown tall. They hold
pink flames in their right hands.
In white from head to foot,
with sidelong, idle look—
in yellow, floating stuff,
black sash and stockings—
touching their avid mouths
with pink sugar on a stick—
like a carnation each holds in her hand—
they mount the lonely street.

The Great Figure

Among the rain
and lights
I saw the figure 5
in gold
on a red
firetruck
moving
tense
unheeded
to gong clangs
siren howls
and wheels rumbling
through the dark city.

By the road to the contagious hospital
under the surge of the blue
mottled clouds driven from the
northeast—a cold wind. Beyond, the
waste of broad, muddy fields
brown with dried weeds, standing and fallen

patches of standing water
the scattering of tall trees

All along the road the reddish
purplish, forked, upstanding, twiggy
stuff of bushes and small trees
with dead, brown leaves under them
leafless vines—

Lifeless in appearance, sluggish
dazed spring approaches—

They enter the new world naked,
cold, uncertain of all
save that they enter. All about them
the cold, familiar wind—

Now the grass, tomorrow
the stiff curl of wildcarrot leaf

One by one objects are defined—
It quickens: clarity, outline of leaf

But now the stark dignity of
entrance—Still, the profound change
has come upon them: rooted, they
grip down and begin to awaken

———

The farmer in deep thought
is pacing through the rain
among his blank fields, with
hands in pockets,
in his head
the harvest already planted.
A cold wind ruffles the water
among the browned weeds.
On all sides
the world rolls coldly away:
black orchards
darkened by the March clouds—
leaving room for thought.
Down past the brushwood
bristling by
the rainsluiced wagonroad
looms the artist figure of
the farmer—composing
—antagonist

The Easter stars are shining
above lights that are flashing—
coronal of the black—
                              Nobody
to say it—
            Nobody to say: pinholes

Thither I would carry her

among the lights—

Burst it asunder
break through to the fifty words
necessary—

                a crown for her head with
castles upon it, skyscrapers
filled with nut-chocolates—

                        dovetame winds—
stars of tinsel
from the great end of a cornucopia
of glass

The rose is obsolete
but each petal ends in
an edge, the double facet
cementing the grooved
columns of air—The edge
cuts without cutting
meets—nothing—renews
itself in metal or porcelain—

whither? It ends—

But if it ends
the start is begun
so that to engage roses
becomes a geometry—

Sharper, neater, more cutting
figured in majolica—
the broken plate
glazed with a rose

Somewhere the sense
makes copper roses
steel roses—

The rose carried weight of love
but love is at an end—of roses

It is at the edge of the
petal that love waits

Crisp, worked to defeat
laboredness—fragile
plucked, moist, half-raised
cold, precise, touching

What

The place between the petal's
edge and the

From the petal's edge a line starts
that being of steel
infinitely fine, infinitely
rigid penetrates
the Milky Way
without contact—lifting
from it—neither hanging
nor pushing—

The fragility of the flower
unbruised
penetrates space

In passing with my mind
on nothing in the world

but the right of way
I enjoy on the road by

virtue of the law—
I saw

an elderly man who
smiled and looked away

to the north past a house—
a woman in blue

who was laughing and
leaning forward to look up

into the man's half
averted face

and a boy of eight who was
looking at the middle of

the man's belly
at a watchchain—

The supreme importance
of this nameless spectacle

sped me by them
without a word—

Why bother where I went?
for I went spinning on the

four wheels of my car
along the wet road until

I saw a girl with one leg
over the rail of a balcony

———

Of death
the barber
the barber
talked to me

cutting my
life with
sleep to trim
my hair—

It's just
a moment
he said, we die
every night—

And of
the newest
ways to grow
hair on

bald death—
I told him
of the quartz
lamp

and of old men
with third
sets of teeth
to the cue

of an old man
who said
at the door—
Sunshine today!

for which
death shaves
him twice
a week

———

O tongue
licking
the sore on
her netherlip

O toppled belly

O passionate cotton
stuck with
matted hair

elysian slobber
upon
the folded handkerchief

I can't die

—moaned the old
jaundiced woman
rolling her
saffron eyeballs

I can't die
I can't die

The pure products of America
go crazy—
mountain folk from Kentucky

or the ribbed north end of
Jersey
with its isolate lakes and

valleys, its deaf-mutes, thieves
old names
and promiscuity between

devil-may-care men who have taken
to railroading
out of sheer lust of adventure—

and young slatterns, bathed
in filth
from Monday to Saturday

to be tricked out that night
with gauds
from imaginations which have no

peasant traditions to give them
character
but flutter and flaunt

sheer rags—succumbing without
emotion
save numbed terror

under some hedge of choke-cherry
or viburnum—
which they cannot express—

Unless it be that marriage
perhaps
with a dash of Indian blood

will throw up a girl so desolate
so hemmed round
with disease or murder

that she'll be rescued by an
agent—
reared by the state and

sent out at fifteen to work in
some hard-pressed
house in the suburbs—

some doctor's family, some Elsie—
voluptuous water
expressing with broken

brain the truth about us—
her great
ungainly hips and flopping breasts

addressed to cheap
jewelry
and rich young men with fine eyes

as if the earth under our feet
were
an excrement of some sky

and we degraded prisoners
destined
to hunger until we eat filth

while the imagination strains
after deer
going by fields of goldenrod in

the stifling heat of September
Somehow
it seems to destroy us

It is only in isolate flecks that
something
is given off

No one
to witness
and adjust, no one to drive the car

———

    so much depends
    upon

    a red wheel
    barrow

    glazed with rain
    water

    beside the white
    chickens

———

Somebody dies every four minutes
in New York State—

To hell with you and your poetry—
You will rot and be blown
through the next solar system
with the rest of the gases—

What the hell do you know about it?

AXIOMS

Don't get killed

Careful Crossing Campaign
Cross Crossings Cautiously

THE HORSES   black
                    &
PRANCED   white

Outings in New York City

Ho for the open country

Don't stay shut up in hot rooms
Go to one of the Great Parks
Pelham Bay for example

It's on Long Island Sound
with bathing, boating
tennis, baseball, golf, etc.

Acres and acres of green grass
wonderful shade trees, rippling brooks

          Take the Pelham Bay Park Branch
          of the Lexington Ave. (East Side)
          Line and you are there in a few
          minutes

Interborough Rapid Transit Co.

The crowd at the ball game
is moved uniformly

by a spirit of uselessness
which delights them—

all the exciting detail
of the chase

and the escape, the error
the flash of genius—

all to no end save beauty
the eternal—

So in detail they, the crowd,
are beautiful

for this
to be warned against

saluted and defied—
It is alive, venomous

it smiles grimly
its words cut—

The flashy female with her
mother, gets it—

The Jew gets it straight—it
is deadly, terrifying—

It is the Inquisition, the
Revolution

It is beauty itself
that lives

day by day in them
idly—

This is
the power of their faces

It is summer, it is the solstice
the crowd is

cheering, the crowd is laughing
in detail

permanently, seriously
without thought

My Luv

My luv
is like
a
greenglass
insulator
on
a blue sky.

The Bull

It is in captivity—
ringed, haltered, chained
to a drag
the bull is godlike

Unlike the cows
he lives alone, nozzles
the sweet grass gingerly
to pass the time away

He kneels, lies down
and stretching out
a foreleg licks himself
about the hoof

then stays
with half-closed eyes,

Olympian commentary on
the bright passage of days.

—The round sun
smooths his lacquer
through
the glossy pinetrees

his substance hard
as ivory or glass—
through which the wind
yet plays—
                    Milkless

he nods
the hair between his horns
and eyes matted
with hyacinthine curls

Fish

It is the whales that drive
the small fish into the fiords.
I have seen forty or fifty
of them in the water at one time.
I have been in a little boat
when the water was boiling
on all sides of us
from them swimming underneath.

The noise of the herring
can be heard nearly a mile.
So thick in the water, they are,
you can't dip the oars in.
All silver!

And all those millions of fish
must be taken, each one, by hand.
The women and children
pull out a little piece
under the throat with their fingers
so that the brine gets inside.

I have seen thousands of barrels
packed with the fish on the shore.

In winter they set the gill-nets
for the cod. Hundreds of them
are caught each night.
In the morning the men
pull in the nets and fish
altogether in the boats.
Cod so big—I have seen—
that when a man held one up
above his head
the tail swept the ground.

Sardines, mackerel, anchovies
all of these. And in the rivers
trout and salmon. I have seen
a net set at the foot of a falls
and in the morning sixty trout in it.

But I guess there are not
such fish in Norway nowadays.

On the Lofoten Islands—
till I was twelve.
Not a tree or a shrub on them.
But in summer
with the sun never gone
the grass is higher than here.

The sun circles the horizon.
Between twelve and one at night
it is very low, near the sea,
to the north. Then
it rises a little, slowly,
till midday, then down again
and so for three months, getting
higher at first, then lower,
until it disappears—

In winter the snow is often
as deep as the ceiling of this room.

If you go there you will see
many Englishmen
near the falls and on the bridges
fishing, fishing.
They will stand there for hours
to catch the fish.

Near the shore
where the water is twenty feet or so
you can see the kingflounders
on the sand. They have
red spots on the side. Men come
in boats and stick them
with long pointed poles.

Have you seen how the Swedes drink tea?
So, in the saucer. They blow it
and turn it this way then that: so.

Tall, gaunt
great drooping nose, eyes dark-circled,
the voice slow and smiling:

I have seen boys stand
where the stream is narrow
a foot each side on two rocks
and grip the trout as they pass through.
They have a special way to hold them,
in the gills, so. The long
fingers arched like grapplehooks.

Then the impatient silence
while a little man said:

The English are great sportsmen.
At the winter resorts
where I stayed
they were always the first up

in the morning, the first
on with the skis.
I once saw a young Englishman
worth seventy million pounds—

You do not know the north.
—and you will see perhaps *huldra*
with long tails
and all blue, from the night,
and the *nekke*, half man and half fish.
When they see one of them
they know some boat will be lost.

The Drunkard

(This poem, recently recovered, was sent by me to my mother in the fall of
1923 accompanied by a letter in part as follows:
    Dearest Mother: Here is a poem to set beside some of my "incomprehen-
sible" latter work. I think you will like this one. It seems the sort of thing
that I am going to do. Art is a curious command. We must do what we are
bidden to do and can go only so far as the light permits. I am always
earnest as you, if anyone, must know. But no doubt I puzzle you—as I do
myself. Plenty of love from your son. W.)

You drunken
tottering
bum

by Christ
in spite of all
your filth

and sordidness
I envy
you

It is the very face
of love
itself

abandoned
in that powerless
committal

to despair

The Dead Baby

Sweep the house
    under the feet of the curious
    holiday seekers—
sweep under the table and the bed
    the baby is dead—

The mother's eyes where she sits
    by the window, unconsoled—
have purple bags under them
    the father—
tall, wellspoken, pitiful
    is the abler of these two—

Sweep the house clean
    here is one who has gone up
    (though problematically)
to heaven, blindly
    by force of the facts—
a clean sweep
    is one way of expressing it—

Hurry up! any minute
    they will be bringing it
    from the hospital—
a white model of our lives
    a curiosity—
surrounded by fresh flowers

Winter

Now the snow
lies on the ground
and more snow
is descending upon it—
Patches of red dirt
hold together
the old
snow patches

This is winter—
rosettes of
leather-green leaves

by the old fence
and bare trees
marking the sky—

This is winter
winter, winter
leather-green leaves
spearshaped
in the falling snow

On Gay Wallpaper

The green-blue ground
is ruled with silver lines
to say the sun is shining

And on this moral sea
of grass or dreams lie flowers
or baskets of desires

Heaven knows what they are
between cerulean shapes
laid regularly round

Mat roses and tridentate
leaves of gold
threes, threes and threes

Three roses and three stems
the basket floating
standing in the horns of blue

Repeated to the ceiling
to the windows
where the day

Blows in
the scalloped curtains to
the sound of rain

The Lily

The branching head of
tiger-lilies through the window
in the air—

A humming bird
is still on whirring wings
above the flowers—

By spotted petals curling back
and tongues that hang
the air is seen—

It's raining—
water's caught
among the curled-back petals

Caught and held
and there's a fly—
are blossoming

9/30   There are no perfect waves—
                Your writings are a sea
                full of misspellings and
                faulty sentences. Level. Troubled.

                A center distant from the land
                touched by the wings
                of nearly silent birds
                that never seem to rest—

                This is the sadness of the sea—
                waves like words, all broken—
                a sameness of lifting and falling mood.

                I lean watching the detail
                of brittle crest, the delicate
                imperfect foam, yellow weed
                one piece like another—

                There is no hope—if not a coral
                island slowly forming
                to wait for birds to drop
                the seeds will make it habitable

10/21   In the dead weeds a rubbish heap
                aflame: the orange flames
                stream horizontal, windblown
                they parallel the ground

waving up and down
the flamepoints alternating
the body streaked with loops
and purple stains while
the pale smoke, above
steadily continues eastward—

What chance have the old?
There are no duties for them
no places where they may sit
their knowledge is laughed at
they cannot see, they cannot hear.
A small bundle on the shoulders
weighs them down
one hand is put back under it
to hold it steady.
Their feet hurt, they are weak
they should not have to suffer
as younger people must and do
there should be a truce for them

10/28   in this strong light
the leafless beechtree
shines like a cloud

it seems to glow
of itself
with a soft stript light

of love
over the brittle
grass

But there are
on second look
a few yellow leaves
still shaking

far apart

just one here one there
trembling vividly

10/29   The justice of poverty
              its shame its dirt
          are one with the meanness
              of love

          its organ in a tarpaulin
              the green birds
          the fat sleepy horse
              the old men

          the grinder sourfaced
              hat over eyes
          the beggar smiling all open
              the lantern out

and the popular tunes—
   sold to the least bidder
for a nickel
   two cents or

nothing at all or even
   against the desire
forced on us

11/1 I won't have to powder my nose tonight 'cause
   Billie's gonna take me home in his car—

   The moon, the dried weeds
   and the Pleiades—

   Seven feet tall
   the dark, dried weedstalks
   make a part of the night
   a red lace
   on the blue milky sky

   Write—
   by a small lamp

   the Pleiades are almost
   nameless
   and the moon is tilted
   and halfgone

And in runningpants and
with ecstatic, æsthetic faces
on the illumined
signboard are leaping
over printed hurdles and
"1/4 of their energy comes from bread"

two
gigantic highschool boys
ten feet tall

11/20   Even idiots grow old
           in a cap with the peak
         over his right ear
           cross-eyed
         shamble-footed
           minding the three goats
         behind the firehouse
           his face is deeper lined
         than last year
           and the rain comes down
         in gusts suddenly

The Moon—

diving
through bedrooms
makes the car
ride upon the page
by virtue of
the law of sentences
Bulleting
through roofs
behind reedy trees
it is the night
waking to
smells of lechery

Child and Vegetables

The fire of the seed is in her pose
upon the clipped lawn, alone

before the old white house
framed in by great elms planted there

symmetrically. Exactly in the center
of this gently sloping scene,

behind her table of squash and green
corn in a pile, facing the road

she sits with feet one by the other
straight and closely pressed

and knees held close, her hands
decorously folded in her lap. Precise

and mild before the vegetables,
the mouth poised in an even smile

of invitation—to come and buy,
the eyes alone appear—half wakened.

These are the lines of a flower-bud's
tight petals, thoughtfully

designed, the vegetable offerings
in a rite. Mutely the smooth globes

of the squash, the cornucopias
of the corn, fresh green, so still,

so aptly made, the whole so full
of peace and symmetry . . .

resting contours of eagerness
and unrest—

The Trees

The trees—being trees
thrash and scream
guffaw and curse—
wholly abandoned
damning the race of men—

Christ, the bastards
haven't even sense enough
to stay out in the rain—

Wha ha ha ha

Wheeeeee
clacka tacka tacka
tacka tacka
wha ha ha ha ha
ha ha ha

knocking knees, buds
bursting from each pore
even the trunk's self
putting out leafheads—

Loose desire!
we naked cry to you—
"Do what you please."

You cannot!

—ghosts
sapped of strength

wailing at the gate
heartbreak at the bridgehead—
desire
dead in the heart

haw haw haw haw
—and memory broken

wheeeeee

There were never satyrs
never maenads
never eagle-headed gods—
These were men
from whose hands sprung
love
bursting the wood—

Trees their companions
—a cold wind winterlong
in the hollows of our flesh
icy with pleasure—

no part of us untouched

The Wind Increases

The harried
earth is swept
          The trees
the tulip's bright
     tips
               sidle and
toss—

          Loose your love
to flow

Blow!

Good Christ what is
a poet—if any
               exists?

a man
whose words will
          bite
                    their way
home—being actual
having the form
               of motion

At each twigtip

new

upon the tortured
body of thought

gripping

the ground

a way
to the last leaftip

The Sea-Elephant

Trundled from
the strangeness of the sea—
a kind of
heaven—

Ladies and Gentlemen!
the greatest
sea-monster ever exhibited
alive

the gigantic
sea-elephant! O wallow
of flesh where
are

there fish enough for
that

appetite stupidity
cannot lessen?

Sick
of April's smallness
the little
leaves—

Flesh has lief of you
enormous sea—
Speak!
Blouaugh! (feed

me) my
flesh is riven—
fish after fish into his maw
unswallowing

to let them glide down
gulching back
half spittle half
brine

the
troubled eyes—torn
from the sea.
(In

a practical voice) They
ought

to put it back where
it came from.

Gape.
Strange head—
told by old sailors—
rising

bearded
to the surface—and
the only
sense out of them

is that woman's
Yes
it's wonderful but they
ought to

put it
back into the sea where
it came from.
Blouaugh!

Swing—ride
walk
on wires—toss balls
stoop and

contort yourselves—
But I
am love. I am
from the sea—

Blouaugh!
there is no crime save
the too-heavy
body

the sea
held playfully—comes
to the surface
the water

boiling
about the head the cows
scattering
fish dripping from

the bounty
of . . . and Spring
they say
Spring is icummen in—

Death

He's dead

the dog won't have to
sleep on his potatoes
any more to keep them
from freezing

he's dead
the old bastard—
He's a bastard because

there's nothing
legitimate in him any
more
        he's dead

He's sick-dead

            he's
a godforsaken curio
without
any breath in it

He's nothing at all
        he's dead

Shrunken up to skin

        Put his head on
one chair and his
feet on another and
he'll lie there
like an acrobat—

Love's beaten. He
beat it. That's why
he's insufferable—

because
he's here needing a
shave and making love
an inside howl
of anguish and defeat—

He's come out of the man
and he's let
the man go—
                    the liar

Dead
          his eyes
rolled up out of
the light—a mockery

                              which
love cannot touch—

just bury it
and hide its face—
for shame.

The Botticellian Trees

The alphabet of
the trees

is fading in the
song of the leaves

the crossing
bars of the thin

letters that spelled
winter

and the cold
have been illumined

with
pointed green

by the rain and sun—
The strict simple

principles of
straight branches

are being modified
by pinched-out

ifs of color, devout
conditions

the smiles of love—
. . . . . .

until the stript
sentences

move as a woman's
limbs under cloth

and praise from secrecy
quick with desire

love's ascendancy
in summer—

In summer the song
sings itself

above the muffled words—

Poem

As the cat
climbed over
the top of

the jamcloset
first the right
forefoot

carefully
then the hind
stepped down

into the pit of
the empty
flowerpot

Nantucket

Flowers through the window
lavender and yellow

changed by white curtains—
Smell of cleanliness—

Sunshine of late afternoon—
On the glass tray

a glass pitcher, the tumbler
turned down, by which

a key is lying—And the
immaculate white bed

This Is Just To Say

I have eaten
the plums
that were in
the icebox

and which
you were probably
saving
for breakfast

Forgive me
they were delicious
so sweet
and so cold

An Early Martyr

Rather than permit him
to testify in court
Giving reasons
why he stole from
Exclusive stores
then sent post-cards
To the police
to come and arrest him
—if they could—
They railroaded him
to an asylum for
The criminally insane
without trial

The prophylactic to
madness
Having been denied him

he went close to
The edge out of
frustration and
Doggedness—

Inflexible, finally they
had to release him—
The institution was
"overcrowded"
They let him go
in the custody of
A relative on condition
that he remain
Out of the state—

They "cured" him all
right
But the set-up
he fought against
Remains—
and his youthful deed
Signalizing
the romantic period
Of a revolt
he served well
Is still good—

Let him be
a factory whistle
That keeps blaring—
Sense, sense, sense!

so long as there's
A mind to remember
and a voice to
carry it on—
Never give up
keep at it!
Unavoided, terrifying
to such bought
Courts as he thought
to trust to but they
Double-crossed him.

Flowers by the Sea

When over the flowery, sharp pasture's
edge, unseen, the salt ocean

lifts its form—chicory and daisies
tied, released, seem hardly flowers alone

but color and the movement—or the shape
perhaps—of restlessness, whereas

the sea is circled and sways
peacefully upon its plantlike stem

To a Poor Old Woman

munching a plum on
the street a paper bag
of them in her hand

They taste good to her
They taste good
to her. They taste
good to her

You can see it by
the way she gives herself
to the one half
sucked out in her hand

Comforted
a solace of ripe plums
seeming to fill the air
They taste good to her

Proletarian Portrait

A big young bareheaded woman
in an apron

Her hair slicked back standing
on the street

One stockinged foot toeing
the sidewalk

Her shoe in her hand. Looking
intently into it

She pulls out the paper insole
to find the nail

That has been hurting her

The Raper from Passenack

was very kind. When she regained
her wits, he said, It's all right, Kid,
I took care of you.

What a mess she was in. Then he added,
You'll never forget me now.
And drove her home.

Only a man who is sick, she said
would do a thing like that.
It must be so.

No one who is not diseased could be
so insanely cruel. He wants to give it
to someone else—

to justify himself. But if I get a
venereal infection out of this
I won't be treated.

I refuse. You'll find me dead in bed
first. Why not? That's
the way she spoke,

I wish I could shoot him. How would
you like to know a murderer?
I may do it.

I'll know by the end of this week.
I wouldn't scream. I bit him
several times

but he was too strong for me.
I can't yet understand it. I don't
faint so easily.

When I came to myself and realized
what had happened all I could do
was to curse

and call him every vile name I could
think of. I was so glad
to be taken home.

I suppose it's my mind—the fear of
infection. I'd rather a million times
have been got pregnant.

But it's the foulness of it can't
be cured. And hatred, hatred of all men
—and disgust.

Genesis

Take some one in England with brains enough
or taste enough, what they call there,
possibly, an aristocrat—tho' seldom enough
And let him get a woman who's bitch enough
with child, then treat her characteristically
enough to make her, having guts enough,
quit the damned place and take a ship to New
York and with the son she got dare enough
to land herself another husband who has also
brains enough to marry her
and take her to St. Thomas where there's room
enough for the sprout to thrive and grow up.

The Yachts

contend in a sea which the land partly encloses
shielding them from the too-heavy blows
of an ungoverned ocean which when it chooses

tortures the biggest hulls, the best man knows
to pit against its beatings, and sinks them pitilessly.
Mothlike in mists, scintillant in the minute

brilliance of cloudless days, with broad bellying sails
they glide to the wind tossing green water
from their sharp prows while over them the crew crawls

ant-like, solicitously grooming them, releasing,
making fast as they turn, lean far over and having
caught the wind again, side by side, head for the mark.

In a well guarded arena of open water surrounded by
lesser and greater craft which, sycophant, lumbering
and flittering follow them, they appear youthful, rare

as the light of a happy eye, live with the grace
of all that in the mind is fleckless, free and
naturally to be desired. Now the sea which holds them

is moody, lapping their glossy sides, as if feeling
for some slightest flaw but fails completely.
Today no race. Then the wind comes again. The yachts

move, jockeying for a start, the signal is set and they
are off. Now the waves strike at them but they are too
well made, they slip through, though they take in canvas.

Arms with hands grasping seek to clutch at the prows.
Bodies thrown recklessly in the way are cut aside.
It is a sea of faces about them in agony, in despair

until the horror of the race dawns staggering the mind,
the whole sea become an entanglement of watery bodies
lost to the world bearing what they cannot hold. Broken,

beaten, desolate, reaching from the dead to be taken up
they cry out, failing, failing! their cries rising
in waves still as the skillful yachts pass over.

Fine Work with Pitch and Copper

Now they are resting
in the fleckless light
separately in unison

like the sacks
of sifted stone stacked
regularly by twos

about the flat roof
ready after lunch
to be opened and strewn

The copper in eight
foot strips has been
beaten lengthwise

down the center at right
angles and lies ready
to edge the coping

One still chewing
picks up a copper strip
and runs his eye along it

St. Francis Einstein of the Daffodils

On the first visit of Professor Einstein to the United States in the spring of 1921.

"Sweet land"
at last!
out of the sea—
the Venusremembering wavelets
rippling with laughter—
freedom
for the daffodils!
—in a tearing wind
that shakes
the tufted orchards—
Einstein, tall as a violet
in the lattice-arbor corner
is tall as
a blossomy peartree

O Samos, Samos
dead and buried. Lesbia
a black cat in the freshturned
garden. All dead.
All flesh they sung
is rotten
Sing of it no longer—
Side by side young and old
take the sun together—
maples, green and red
yellowbells
and the vermilion quinceflower
together—

The peartree
with fœtid blossoms
sways its high topbranches
with contrary motions
and there are both pinkflowered
and coralflowered peachtrees
in the bare chickenyard
of the old negro
with white hair who hides
poisoned fish-heads
here and there
where stray cats find them—
find them

Spring days
swift and mutable
winds blowing four ways
hot and cold
shaking the flowers—
Now the northeast wind
moving in fogs leaves the grass
cold and dripping. The night
is dark. But in the night
the southeast wind approaches.
The owner of the orchard
lies in bed
with open windows
and throws off his covers
one by one

Advent of Today

South wind
striking in—torn
spume—trees

inverted over trees
scudding low
a sea become winged

bringing today
out of yesterday
in bursts of rain—

a darkened presence
above
detail of October grasses

veiled at once
in a downpour—
conflicting rattle of

the rain against
the storm's slow majesty—
leaves

rising
instead of falling
the sun

coming and going
toward the
middle parts of the sky

Classic Scene

A power-house
in the shape of
a red brick chair
90 feet high

on the seat of which
sit the figures
of two metal
stacks—aluminum—

commanding an area
of squalid shacks
side by side—
from one of which

buff smoke
streams while under
a grey sky
the other remains

passive today—

Autumn

A stand of people
by an open

grave underneath
the heavy leaves

celebrates
the cut and fill

for the new road
where

an old man
on his knees

reaps a basket-
ful of

matted grasses for
his goats

The Term

A rumpled sheet
of brown paper
about the length

and apparent bulk
of a man was
rolling with the

wind slowly over
and over in
the street as

a car drove down
upon it and
crushed it to

the ground. Unlike
a man it rose
again rolling

with the wind over
and over to be as
it was before.

The Poor

It's the anarchy of poverty
delights me, the old
yellow wooden house indented
among the new brick tenements

Or a cast-iron balcony
with panels showing oak branches

in full leaf. It fits
the dress of the children

reflecting every stage and
custom of necessity—
Chimneys, roofs, fences of
wood and metal in an unfenced

age and enclosing next to
nothing at all: the old man
in a sweater and soft black
hat who sweeps the sidewalk—

his own ten feet of it—
in a wind that fitfully
turning his corner has
overwhelmed the entire city

Between Walls

the back wings
of the

hospital where
nothing

will grow lie
cinders

in which shine
the broken

pieces of a green
bottle

Middle

of this profusion
a robin flies carrying
food on its tongue
and a flag

red white and
blue hangs
motionless. Return
from the sick

wean the mind
again from among
the foliage also of
infection. There

is a brass band at
the monument
and the children
that paraded

the blistering streets
are giving lustily
to the memory
of our war dead.

Remain and listen or
use up the time
perhaps
among the side streets

watching the elms
and rhododendrons the
peonies and
changeless laurels.

These

are the desolate, dark weeks
when nature in its barrenness
equals the stupidity of man.

The year plunges into night
and the heart plunges
lower than night

to an empty, windswept place
without sun, stars or moon
but a peculiar light as of thought

that spins a dark fire—
whirling upon itself until,
in the cold, it kindles

to make a man aware of nothing
that he knows, not loneliness
itself—Not a ghost but

would be embraced—emptiness,
despair—(They
whine and whistle) among

the flashes and booms of war;
houses of whose rooms
the cold is greater than can be thought,

the people gone that we loved,
the beds lying empty, the couches
damp, the chairs unused—

Hide it away somewhere
out of the mind, let it get roots
and grow, unrelated to jealous

ears and eyes—for itself.
In this mine they come to dig—all.
Is this the counterfoil to sweetest

music? The source of poetry that
seeing the clock stopped, says,
The clock has stopped

that ticked yesterday so well?
and hears the sound of lakewater
splashing—that is now stone.

The Last Words of My English Grandmother

There were some dirty plates
and a glass of milk
beside her on a small table
near the rank, disheveled bed—

Wrinkled and nearly blind
she lay and snored
rousing with anger in her tones
to cry for food,

Gimme something to eat—
They're starving me—
I'm all right—I won't go
to the hospital. No, no, no

Give me something to eat!
Let me take you
to the hospital, I said
and after you are well

you can do as you please.
She smiles, Yes

you do what you please first
then I can do what I please—

Oh, oh, oh! she cried
as the ambulance men lifted
her to the stretcher—
Is this what you call

making me comfortable?
By now her mind was clear—
Oh you think you're smart
you young people,

she said, but I'll tell you
you don't know anything.
Then we started.
On the way

we passed a long row
of elms. She looked at them
awhile out of
the ambulance window and said,

What are all those
fuzzy-looking things out there?
Trees? Well, I'm tired
of them and rolled her head away.

River Rhyme

The rumpled river
takes its course
lashed by rain

This is that now
that tortures
skeletons of weeds

and muddy waters
eat their
banks the drain

of swamps a bulk
that writhes and fat-
tens as it speeds.

The End of the Parade

The sentence undulates
raising no song—
It is too old, the
words of it are falling
apart. Only percussion
strokes continue
with weakening
emphasis what was once
cadenced melody
full of sweet breath.

River Rhyme II

Shine miraculous
mottled river
dancing flames
patched black with
doom. We shall
never see what our
love portends
never its flower
in bloom.

Election Day

Warm sun, quiet air
an old man sits

in the doorway of
a broken house—

boards for windows
plaster falling

from between the stones
and strokes the head

of a spotted dog

Passaic, N.J.

I'd like to live on Tulip Street
and have a fig tree in the yard
I'd wrap it in tarpaper and rags
lest the winter prove too hard

The niggers and wops on Tulip Street
have few prejudices, I none
and fig trees grow freely there
for practically anyone.

Gothic Candor

You have such a way of talking of Him!
and his little fifteen year old mother!

She was never a tragic figure, you say.
I feel sorry for them. They were pathetic.

I pity them. And I wonder if those sculptors
ever really looked at a woman holding

a baby in her arms. Oh see this one! I'm
so glad he made Him a jew! And look at her

face! That's the way He was when He was
here with us, just a little Jewish baby!

A Sort of a Song

Let the snake wait under
his weed
and the writing
be of words, slow and quick, sharp
to strike, quiet to wait,
sleepless.

—through metaphor to reconcile
the people and the stones.
Compose. (No ideas
but in things) Invent!
Saxifrage is my flower that splits
the rocks.

Paterson: The Falls

What common language to unravel?
The Falls, combed into straight lines
from that rafter of a rock's
lip. Strike in! the middle of

some trenchant phrase, some
well packed clause. Then . . .
This is my plan. 4 sections: First,
the archaic persons of the drama.

An eternity of bird and bush,
resolved. An unraveling:
the confused streams aligned, side
by side, speaking! Sound

married to strength, a strength
of falling—from a height! The wild
voice of the shirt-sleeved
Evangelist rivaling, Hear

me! I am the Resurrection
and the Life! echoing
among the bass and pickerel, slim
eels from Barbados, Sargasso

Sea, working up the coast to that
bounty, ponds and wild streams—
Third, the old town: Alexander Hamilton
working up from St. Croix,

from that sea! and a deeper, whence
he came! stopped cold
by that unmoving roar, fastened
there: the rocks silent

but the water, married to the stone,
voluble, though frozen; the water
even when and though frozen
still whispers and moans—

And in the brittle air
a factory bell clangs, at dawn, and
snow whines under their feet. Fourth,
the modern town, a

disembodied roar! the cataract and
its clamor broken apart—and from
all learning, the empty
ear struck from within, roaring . . .

The Dance

In Brueghel's great picture, The Kermess,
the dancers go round, they go round and
around, the squeal and the blare and the
tweedle of bagpipes, a bugle and fiddles
tipping their bellies (round as the thick-
sided glasses whose wash they impound)
their hips and their bellies off balance
to turn them. Kicking and rolling about
the Fair Grounds, swinging their butts, those
shanks must be sound to bear up under such
rollicking measures, prance as they dance
in Brueghel's great picture, The Kermess.

Burning the Christmas Greens

Their time past, pulled down
cracked and flung to the fire
—go up in a roar

All recognition lost, burnt clean
clean in the flame, the green
dispersed, a living red,
flame red, red as blood wakes
on the ash—

and ebbs to a steady burning
the rekindled bed become
a landscape of flame

At the winter's midnight
we went to the trees, the coarse
holly, the balsam and
the hemlock for their green

At the thick of the dark
the moment of the cold's
deepest plunge we brought branches
cut from the green trees

to fill our need, and over
doorways, about paper Christmas
bells covered with tinfoil
and fastened by red ribbons

we stuck the green prongs
in the windows hung
woven wreaths and above pictures
the living green. On the

mantle we built a green forest
and among those hemlock
sprays put a herd of small
white deer as if they

were walking there. All this!
and it seemed gentle and good
to us. Their time past,
relief! The room bare. We

stuffed the dead grate
with them upon the half burnt out
log's smoldering eye, opening
red and closing under them

and we stood there looking down.
Green is a solace
a promise of peace, a fort
against the cold (though we

did not say so) a challenge
above the snow's
hard shell. Green (we might
have said) that, where

small birds hide and dodge
and lift their plaintive

rallying cries, blocks for them
and knocks down

the unseeing bullets of
the storm. Green spruce boughs
pulled down by a weight of
snow—Transformed!

Violence leaped and appeared.
Recreant! roared to life
as the flame rose through and
our eyes recoiled from it.

In the jagged flames green
to red, instant and alive. Green!
those sure abutments . . . Gone!
lost to mind

and quick in the contracting
tunnel of the grate
appeared a world! Black
mountains, black and red—as

yet uncolored—and ash white,
an infant landscape of shimmering
ash and flame and we, in
that instant, lost,

breathless to be witnesses,
as if we stood
ourselves refreshed among
the shining fauna of that fire.

Raleigh Was Right

We cannot go to the country
for the country will bring us
    no peace
What can the small violets tell us
that grow on furry stems in
the long grass among lance shaped
    leaves?

Though you praise us
and call to mind the poets
who sung of our loveliness
it was long ago!
long ago! when country people
would plow and sow with
flowering minds and pockets
    at ease—
if ever this were true.

Not now. Love itself a flower
with roots in a parched ground.
Empty pockets make empty heads.
Cure it if you can but

do not believe that we can live
today in the country
for the country will bring us
    no peace.

To Ford Madox Ford in Heaven

Is it any better in Heaven, my friend Ford,
    than you found it in Provence?

I don't think so for you made Provence a
    heaven by your praise of it
to give a foretaste of what might be
    your joy in the present circumstances.
It was Heaven you were describing there
    transubstantiated from its narrowness
to resemble the paths and gardens of a
    greater world where you now reside.
But, dear man, you have taken a major
    part of it from us.
            Provence that you
praised so well will never be the same
    Provence to us
        now you are gone.

A heavenly man you seem to me now, never
    having been for me a saintly one.
It lived about you, a certain grossness that
    was not like the world.
The world is cleanly, polished and well
    made but heavenly man
is filthy with his flesh and corrupt that
    loves to eat and drink and whore—
to laugh at himself and not be afraid of
    himself knowing well he has

no possessions and opinions that are worth
    caring a broker's word about
and that all he is, but one thing, he feeds
    as one will feed a pet dog.

So roust and love and dredge the belly full
    in Heaven's name!
I laugh to think of you wheezing in Heaven.
    Where is Heaven? But why
do I ask that, since you showed the way?
    I don't care a damn for it
other than for that better part lives beside
    me here so long as I
live and remember you. Thank God you
    were not delicate, you let the world in
and lied! damn it you lied grossly
    sometimes. But it was all, I
see now, a carelessness, the part of a man
    that is homeless here on earth.

Provence, the fat assed Ford will never
    again strain the chairs of your cafés
pull and pare for his dish your sacred garlic,
    grunt and sweat and lick
his lips. Gross as the world he has left to
    us he has become
a part of that of which you were the known
    part, Provence, he loved so well.

A Woman in Front of a Bank

The bank is a matter of columns,
like . convention,
unlike invention; but the pediments
sit there in the sun

to convince the doubting of
investments "solid
as rock"—upon which the world
stands, the world of finance,

the only world: Just there,
talking with another woman while
rocking a baby carriage
back and forth stands a woman in

a pink cotton dress, bare legged
and headed whose legs
are two columns to hold up
her face, like Lenin's (her loosely

arranged hair profusely blond) or
Darwin's and there you
have it:
a woman in front of a bank.

When Structure Fails
Rhyme Attempts to Come to the Rescue

The old horse dies slow.
By gradual degrees
the fervor of his veins
matches the leaves'

stretch, day by day. But
the pace that his
mind keeps is the pace
of his dreams. He

does what he can, with
unabated phlegm,
ahem! but the pace that
his flesh keeps—

leaning, leaning upon
the bars—beggars
by far all pace and every
refuge of his dreams.

Threnody

The Christian coin—
embossed with a dove and sword—
is not wasted by war,
rather it thrives on it

and should be tossed
into the sea for the fish
to eye it as it falls
past the clutching fingers
of children—
for them to eye it
and sing, join in a choir
to rival the land and set
coral branches swaying:
Peace, peace to the oceans,
the dread hurricane die,
ice melt at the poles
and sharks be at rest!
as it drops, lost, to its grave.

East Coocoo

The innocent locomotive
laboring against the grade
streams its cloud of smoke
above the fallen snow.

Its labors are human to
the superhuman dread that
fastens every mind upon
the coming blast of bombs.

Peacefully we quarrel
over the doctrinal wage-rate,

build the cathedral, split
hairs in internecine wars.

And we too shall die
among the rest and the brave
locomotive stand falling apart
untended for a thousand years.

The Woodpecker

Innocence! Innocence is the condition of heaven.
Only in that which we do not yet know shall we
be fêted, fed. That is to say, with ceremony. The
unknown is our refuge toward which we hurtle. For
even tho', lacking parachute, we be flattened
upon the earth it will not be the same earth we left
to fly upward. To seek what? There is nothing
there. It is not even the unknown for us now. But
we never knew the earth so solidly as when we were
crushed upon it. From a height we fall, innocent,
to our deaths.

I'd rather in the November be a
woodpecker of the woods. A cry, a movement,
red dabbled, among the bare branches. A light, a
destination where destinations are endless and
the beetle the end of flight. Fed and the ceremony
unwitnessed other than by the lichened rocks, the
dry leaves and the upright bodies of the trees.

It is innocence flings the black and white body
through the air, innocence guides him. Flight
means only desire and desire the end of flight,
stabbing there with a barbed tongue which *succeeds!*

Passer Domesticus

Shabby little bird
I suppose it's
the story every-
where, if you're

domestic you're drab.
Peep peep!
the nightingale
's your cousin but

these flagrant
amours get you no-

where. Dull
to the eye you have

crept in unmolested.

The Descent

The descent beckons
        as the ascent beckoned.
                Memory is a kind
of accomplishment,
        a sort of renewal
            even
an initiation, since the spaces it opens are new places
        inhabited by hordes
              heretofore unrealized,
of new kinds—
        since their movements
              are toward new objectives
(even though formerly they were abandoned).

No defeat is made up entirely of defeat—since
the world it opens is always a place
        formerly
            unsuspected. A
world lost,
        a world unsuspected,
              beckons to new places
and no whiteness (lost) is so white as the memory
of whiteness   .

With evening, love wakens
        though its shadows
              which are alive by reason
of the sun shining—
        grow sleepy now and drop away
            from desire   .

Love without shadows stirs now
                beginning to awaken
                                as night
advances.

The descent
                made up of despairs
                                and without accomplishment
realizes a new awakening:
                                which is a reversal
of despair.
                For what we cannot accomplish, what
is denied to love,
                what we have lost in the anticipation—
                                a descent follows,
endless and indestructible   .

To a Dog Injured in the Street

It is myself,
                not the poor beast lying there
                                yelping with pain
that brings me to myself with a start—
                as at the explosion
                                of a bomb, a bomb that has laid
all the world waste.
                I can do nothing
                                but sing about it
and so I am assuaged
                from my pain.

A drowsy numbness drowns my sense
                as if of hemlock
                                I had drunk. I think
of the poetry
                of René Char
                                and all he must have seen
and suffered
                that has brought him
                                to speak only of
sedgy rivers,
                of daffodils and tulips
                                whose roots they water,
even to the free-flowing river
                that laves the rootlets
                                of those sweet-scented flowers
that people the
                milky

                                way   .

I remember Norma
                our English setter of my childhood
                                her silky ears
and expressive eyes.
                She had a litter
                                of pups one night
in our pantry and I kicked
                one of them
                                thinking, in my alarm,
that they
                were biting her breasts
                                to destroy her.

I remember also
            a dead rabbit
                        lying harmlessly
on the outspread palm
            of a hunter's hand.
                        As I stood by
watching
            he took a hunting knife
                        and with a laugh
thrust it
            up into the animal's private parts.
                        I almost fainted.

Why should I think of that now?
            The cries of a dying dog
                        are to be blotted out
as best I can.
            René Char
                        you are a poet who believes
in the power of beauty
            to right all wrongs.
                        I believe it also.
With invention and courage
            we shall surpass
                        the pitiful dumb beasts,
let all men believe it,
            as you have taught me also
                        to believe it.

The Yellow Flower

What shall I say, because talk I must?
          That I have found a cure
               for the sick?
I have found no cure
          for the sick   .
               but this crooked flower
which only to look upon
          all men
               are cured. This
is that flower
          for which all men
               sing secretly their hymns
of praise. This
          is that sacred
               flower!

Can this be so?
          A flower so crooked
               and obscure? It is
a mustard flower
          and not a mustard flower,
               a single spray
topping the deformed stem
          of fleshy leaves
               in this freezing weather
under glass.

An ungainly flower and
            an unnatural one,
                        in this climate; what
can be the reason
            that it has picked me out
                        to hold me, openmouthed,
rooted before this window
            in the cold,
                        my will
drained from me
            so that I have only eyes
                        for these yellow,
twisted petals   .   ?

That the sight,
            though strange to me,
                        must be a common one,
is clear: there are such flowers
            with such leaves
                        native to some climate
which they can call
            their own.

But why the torture
            and the escape through
                        the flower? It is
as if Michelangelo
            had conceived the subject
                        of his *Slaves* from this
—or might have done so.
            And did he not make
                        the marble bloom? I

am sad
                as he was sad
                                in his heroic mood.
But also
                I have eyes
                                that are made to see and if
they see ruin for myself
                and all that I hold
                                dear, they see
also
                through the eyes
                                and through the lips
and tongue the power
                to free myself
                                and speak of it, as
Michelangelo through his hands
                had the same, if greater,
                                power.

Which leaves, to account for,
                the tortured bodies
                                of
the slaves themselves
                and
                                the tortured body of my flower
which is not a mustard flower at all
                but some unrecognized
                                and unearthly flower
for me to naturalize
                and acclimate
                                and choose it for my own.

The Artist

Mr. T.
           bareheaded
                        in a soiled undershirt
his hair standing out
           on all sides
                        stood on his toes
heels together
           arms gracefully
                        for the moment
curled above his head.
           Then he whirled about
                        bounded
into the air
           and with an *entrechat*
                        perfectly achieved
completed the figure.
           My mother
                        taken by surprise
where she sat
           in her invalid's chair
                        was left speechless.
Bravo! she cried at last
           and clapped her hands.
                        The man's wife
came from the kitchen:
           What goes on here? she said.
                        But the show was over.

Theocritus: Idyl I

A Version from the Greek

THYRSIS
The whisper of the wind in
        that pine tree,
                goatherd,
is sweet as the murmur of live water;
        likewise
                your flute notes. After Pan
you shall bear away second prize.
        And if he
                take the goat
with the horns,
        the she-goat
                is yours: but if
he choose the she-goat,
        the kid will fall
                to your lot.
And the flesh of the kid
        is dainty
                before they begin milking them.

GOATHERD
Your song is sweeter,
        shepherd,
                than the music
of the water as it plashes
        from the high face
                of yonder rock!

If the Muses
            choose the young ewe
                        you shall receive
a stall-fed lamb
            as your reward,
                        but if
they prefer the lamb
            you
                        shall have the ewe for
                        second prize.

THYRSIS
Will you not, goatherd,
            in the Nymph's name
                        take your place on this
                        sloping knoll
among the tamarisks
            and pipe for me
                        while I tend my sheep.

GOATHERD
No, shepherd,
            nothing doing;
                        it's not for us
to be heard during the noon hush.
            We dread Pan,
                        who for a fact
is stretched out somewhere,
            dog tired from the chase;
                        his mood is bitter,
anger ready at his nostrils.

But, Thyrsis,
                    since you are good at
singing of *The Afflictions of Daphnis*,
                    and have most deeply
                              meditated the pastoral mode,
come here,
               let us sit down,
                         under this elm
facing Priapus and the fountain fairies,
                    here where the shepherds come
                                        to try themselves out
by the oak trees.
                    Ah! may you sing
                              as you sang that day
facing Chromis out of Libya,
               I will let you milk, yes,
                         three times over,
a goat that is the mother of twins
                    and even when
                              she has sucked her kids
her milk fills
               two pails. I will give besides,
                         new made, a two-eared bowl
of ivy-wood,
               rubbed with beeswax
                         that smacks still
of the knife of the carver.
               Round its upper edges
                         winds the ivy, ivy

flecked with yellow flowers
        and about it
                is twisted
a tendril joyful with the saffron fruit.
        Within,
                is limned a girl,
as fair a thing as the gods have made,
        dressed in a sweeping
                gown.
Her hair
        is confined by a snood.
                Beside her
two fair-haired youths
        with alternate speech
                are contending
but her heart is
        untouched.
                Now,
she glances at one,
        smiling,
                and now, lightly
she flings the other a thought,
        while their eyes,
                by reason of love's
long vigils, are heavy
        but their labors
                all in vain.
In addition
        there is fashioned there
                an ancient fisherman

and a rock,
        a rugged rock,
                on which
with might and main
        the old man poises a great net
            for the cast
as one who puts his whole heart into it.
        One would say
            that he was fishing
with the full strength of his limbs
        so big do his muscles stand out
            about the neck.
Gray-haired though he be,
        he has the strength
            of a young man.
Now, separated
        from the sea-broken old man
            by a narrow interval
is a vineyard,
        heavy
            with fire-red clusters,
and on a rude wall
        sits a small boy
            guarding them.
Round him
        two she-foxes are skulking.
        One
goes the length of the vine-rows
        to eat the grapes
            while the other

brings all her cunning to bear,
        by what has been set down,
           vowing
she will never quit the lad
        until
           she leaves him bare
and breakfastless.
        But the boy
           is plaiting a pretty
cage of locust stalks and asphodel,
        fitting in the reeds
           and cares less for his scrip
and the vines
        than he takes delight
           in his plaiting.
All about the cup
        is draped the mild acanthus
           a miracle of varied work,
a thing for you to marvel at.
        I paid
           a Caledonian ferryman
a goat and a great white
        cream-cheese
           for the bowl.
It is still virgin to me,
        its lip has never touched mine.
           To gain my desire,
I would gladly
        give this cup
           if you, my friend,

will sing for me
                that delightful song.
                                I hold nothing back.
Begin, my friend,
                for you cannot,
                                you may be sure,
take your song,
                which drives all things out of mind,
                                with you to the other world.

A Negro Woman

carrying a bunch of marigolds
                wrapped
                                in an old newspaper:
She carries them upright,
                bareheaded,
                                the bulk
of her thighs
                causing her to waddle
                                as she walks
looking into
                the store window which she passes
                                on her way.
What is she
                but an ambassador
                                from another world
a world of pretty marigolds
                of two shades
                                which she announces

not knowing what she does
             other
                        than walk the streets
holding the flowers upright
             as a torch
                        so early in the morning.

To a Man Dying on His Feet

—not that we are not all
             "dying on our feet"
                        but the look you give me
and to which I bow,
             is more immediate.
                        It is keenly alert,
suspicious of me—
             as of all that are living—and
                        apologetic.
Your jaw
             wears the stubble
                        of a haggard beard,
a dirty beard,
             which resembles
                        the snow through which
your long legs
             are conducting you.
                        Whither? Where are you going?
This would be a fine day
             to go on a journey.
                        Say to Florida

where at this season
        all go
                nowadays.
There grows the hibiscus,
        the star jasmine
                and more than I can tell
but the odors
        from what I know
                must be alluring.
Come with me there!
        you look like a good guy,
                come this evening.
The plane leaves at 6:30
        or have you another
                appointment?

The Pink Locust

I'm persistent as the pink locust,
        once admitted
                to the garden,
you will not easily get rid of it.
        Tear it from the ground,
                if one hair-thin rootlet
remain
        it will come again.
                It is
flattering to think of myself
        so. It is also
                laughable.

A modest flower,
        resembling a pink sweet-pea,
            you cannot help
but admire it
        until its habits
            become known.
Are we not most of us
        like that? It would be
            too much
if the public
        pried among the minutiae
            of our private affairs.
Not
        that we have anything to hide
            but could *they*
stand it? Of course
        the world would be gratified
            to find out
what fools we have made of ourselves.
        The question is,
            would they
be generous with us—
        as we have been
            with others? It is,
as I say,
        a flower
            incredibly resilient
under attack!
        Neglect it
            and it will grow into a tree.

I wish I could so think of myself
                  and of what
                                  is to become of me.
The poet himself,
                  what does he think of himself
                                  facing his world?
It will not do to say,
                  as he is inclined to say:
                                  Not much. The poem
would be in *that* betrayed.
                  He might as well answer—
                                  "a rose is a rose
is a rose" and let it go at that.
                  A rose *is* a rose
                                  and the poem equals it
if it be well made.
                  The poet
                                  cannot slight himself
without slighting
                  his poem—
                                  which would be
ridiculous.
                  Life offers
                                  no greater reward.
And so,
                  like this flower,
                                  I persist—
for what there may be in it.
                  I am not,
                                  I know,

in the galaxy of poets
           a rose
                    but *who*, among the rest,
will deny me
           my place.

BOOK I

Of asphodel, that greeny flower,
           like a buttercup
                    upon its branching stem—
save that it's green and wooden—
           I come, my sweet,
                    to sing to you.
We lived long together
           a life filled,
                    if you will,
with flowers. So that
           I was cheered
                    when I came first to know
that there were flowers also
           in hell.
                    Today
I'm filled with the fading memory of those flowers
           that we both loved,
                    even to this poor
colorless thing—
           I saw it
                    when I was a child—

little prized among the living
        but the dead see,
                asking among themselves:
What do I remember
        that was shaped
                as this thing is shaped?
while our eyes fill
        with tears.
                Of love, abiding love
it will be telling
        though too weak a wash of crimson
        colors it
to make it wholly credible.
        There is something
                something urgent
I have to say to you
        and you alone
                but it must wait
while I drink in
        the joy of your approach,
                perhaps for the last time.
And so
        with fear in my heart
                I drag it out
and keep on talking
        for I dare not stop.
                Listen while I talk on
against time.
        It will not be
                for long.

I have forgot   .
              and yet I see clearly enough
                    something
central to the sky
              which ranges round it.
                    An odor
springs from it!
              A sweetest odor!
                    Honeysuckle! And now
there comes the buzzing of a bee!
              and a whole flood
                    of sister memories!
Only give me time,
              time to recall them
                    before I shall speak out.
Give me time,
              time.
When I was a boy
              I kept a book
                    to which, from time
to time,
              I added pressed flowers
                    until, after a time,
I had a good collection.
              The asphodel,
                    forebodingly,
among them.
              I bring you,
                    reawakened,
a memory of those flowers.
              They were sweet
                    when I pressed them

and retained
>   something of their sweetness
>   a long time.
It is a curious odor,
>   a moral odor,
>   that brings me
near to you.
>   The color
>   was the first to go.
There had come to me
>   a challenge,
>   your dear self,
mortal as I was,
>   the lily's throat
>   to the hummingbird!
Endless wealth,
>   I thought,
>   held out its arms to me.
A thousand tropics
>   in an apple blossom.
>   The generous earth itself
gave us lief.
>   The whole world
>   became my garden!
But the sea
>   which no one tends
>   is also a garden
when the sun strikes it
>   and the waves
>   are wakened.

I have seen it
            and so have you
                        when it puts all flowers
to shame.
            Too, there are the starfish
                        stiffened by the sun
and other sea wrack
            and weeds. We knew that
                        along with the rest of it
for we were born by the sea,
            knew its rose hedges
                        to the very water's brink.
There the pink mallow grows
            and in their season
                        strawberries
and there, later,
            we went to gather
                        the wild plum.
I cannot say
            that I have gone to hell
                        for your love
but often
            found myself there
                        in your pursuit.
I do not like it
            and wanted to be
                        in heaven. Hear me out.
Do not turn away.
I have learned much in my life
            from books
                        and out of them
about love.

Death
                    is not the end of it.
There is a hierarchy
                    which can be attained,
                            I think,
in its service.
                    Its guerdon
                            is a fairy flower;
a cat of twenty lives.
                    If no one came to try it
                            the world
would be the loser.
                    It has been
                            for you and me
as one who watches a storm
                    come in over the water.
                            We have stood
from year to year
                    before the spectacle of our lives
                            with joined hands.
The storm unfolds.
                    Lightning
                            plays about the edges of the
                            clouds.
The sky to the north
                    is placid,
                            blue in the afterglow
as the storm piles up.
                    It is a flower
                            that will soon reach
the apex of its bloom.

We danced,
                    in our minds,
and read a book together.
                    You remember?
                              It was a serious book.
And so books
          entered our lives.
The sea! The sea!
          Always
                    when I think of the sea
there comes to mind
          the *Iliad*
                    and Helen's public fault
that bred it.
          Were it not for that
                    there would have been
no poem but the world
          if we had remembered,
                    those crimson petals
spilled among the stones,
          would have called it simply
                    murder.
The sexual orchid that bloomed then
          sending so many
                    disinterested
men to their graves
          has left its memory
                    to a race of fools
or heroes
          if silence is a virtue.
                    The sea alone

with its multiplicity
        holds any hope.
                The storm
has proven abortive
        but we remain
                after the thoughts it roused
to
        re-cement our lives.
                It is the mind
the mind
        that must be cured
                short of death's
intervention,
        and the will becomes again
                a garden. The poem
is complex and the place made
        in our lives
                for the poem.
Silence can be complex too,
        but you do not get far
                with silence.
Begin again.
        It is like Homer's
                catalogue of ships:
it fills up the time.
        I speak in figures,
                well enough, the dresses
you wear are figures also,
        we could not meet
                otherwise. When I speak

of flowers
                    it is to recall
                    that at one time
we were young.
                    All women are not Helen,
                    I know that,
but have Helen in their hearts.
                    My sweet,
                    you have it also, therefore
I love you
                    and could not love you otherwise.
                    Imagine you saw
a field made up of women
                    all silver-white.
                    What should you do
but love them?
                    The storm bursts
                    or fades! it is not
the end of the world.
                    Love is something else,
                    or so I thought it,
a garden which expands,
                    though I knew you as a woman
                    and never thought otherwise,
until the whole sea
                    has been taken up
                    and all its gardens.
It was the love of love,
                    the love that swallows up all else,
                    a grateful love,

a love of nature, of people,
                animals,
                                a love engendering
gentleness and goodness
                that moved me
                                and *that* I saw in you.
I should have known,
                though I did not,
                                that the lily-of-the-valley
is a flower makes many ill
                who whiff it.
                                We had our children,
rivals in the general onslaught.
                I put them aside
                                though I cared for them
as well as any man
                could care for his children
                                according to my lights.
You understand
                I had to meet you
                                after the event
and have still to meet you.
                Love
                                to which you too shall bow
along with me—
                a flower
                                a weakest flower
shall be our trust
                and not because
                                we are too feeble

to do otherwise
>>but because
>>>>at the height of my power
I risked what I had to do,
>>therefore to prove
>>>>that we love each other
while my very bones sweated
>>that I could not cry to you
>>>>in the act.
Of asphodel, that greeny flower,
>>I come, my sweet,
>>>>to sing to you!
My heart rouses
>>thinking to bring you news
>>>>of something
that concerns you
>>and concerns many men. Look at
>>>>what passes for the new.
You will not find it there but in
>>despised poems.
>>>>It is difficult
to get the news from poems
>>yet men die miserably every day
>>>>for lack
of what is found there.
>>Hear me out
>>>>for I too am concerned
and every man
>>who wants to die at peace in his bed
>>>>besides.

CODA

Inseparable from the fire
            its light
                        takes precedence over it.
Then follows
            what we have dreaded—
                        but it can never
overcome what has gone before.
            In the huge gap
                        between the flash
and the thunderstroke
            spring has come in
                        or a deep snow fallen.
Call it old age.
            In that stretch
                        we have lived to see
a colt kick up his heels.
            Do not hasten
                        laugh and play
in an eternity
            the heat will not overtake the light.
                        That's sure.
That gelds the bomb,
            permitting
                        that the mind contain it.
This is that interval,
            that sweetest interval,
                        when love will blossom,
come early, come late
            and give itself to the lover.
Only the imagination is real!

I have declared it
time without end.
If a man die
it is because death
has first
possessed his imagination.
But if he refuse death—
no greater evil
can befall him
unless it be the death of love
meet him
in full career.
Then indeed
for him
the light has gone out.
But love and the imagination
are of a piece,
swift as the light
to avoid destruction.
So we come to watch time's flight
as we might watch
summer lightning
or fireflies, secure,
by grace of the imagination,
safe in its care.
For if
the light itself
has escaped,
the whole edifice opposed to it
goes down.

Light, the imagination
                and love,
                        in our age,
by natural law,
                which we worship,
                        maintain
all of a piece
                their dominance.
So let us love
                confident as is the light
                        in its struggle with darkness
that there is as much to say
                and more
                        for the one side
and that not the darker
                which John Donne
                        for instance
among many men
                presents to us.
                        In the controversy
touching the younger
                and the older Tolstoy,
                        Villon, St. Anthony, Kung,
Rimbaud, Buddha
                and Abraham Lincoln
                        the palm goes
always to the light;
                who most shall advance the light—
                        call it what you may!

The light
        for all time shall outspeed
                the thunder crack.
Medieval pageantry
        is human and we enjoy
                the rumor of it
as in our world we enjoy
        the reading of Chaucer,
                likewise
a priest's raiment
        (or that of a savage chieftain).
                It is all
a celebration of the light.
        All the pomp and ceremony
                of weddings,
"Sweet Thames, run softly
        till I end
                my song,"—
are of an equal sort.
For our wedding, too,
        the light was wakened
                and shone. The light!
the light stood before us
        waiting!
                I thought the world
stood still.
        At the altar
                so intent was I
before my vows,
        so moved by your presence
                a girl so pale

and ready to faint
        that I pitied
                and wanted to protect you.
As I think of it now,
        after a lifetime,
                it is as if
a sweet-scented flower
        were poised
                and for me did open.
Asphodel
        has no odor
                save to the imagination
but it too
        celebrates the light.
                It is late
but an odor
        as from our wedding
                has revived for me
and begun again to penetrate
        into all crevices
                of my world.

Sappho

That man is peer of the gods, who
face to face sits listening
to your sweet speech and lovely
        laughter.

It is this that rouses a tumult
in my breast. At mere sight of you
my voice falters, my tongue
                    is broken.

Straightway, a delicate fire runs in
my limbs; my eyes
are blinded and my ears
                    thunder.

Sweat pours out: a trembling hunts
me down. I grow
paler than grass and lack little
                    of dying.

Greeting for Old Age

Advance and take your place:
how do you do?
I salute you along with your half-blind

sister whom I know intimately
related by your cryptic smile.

I saw you approaching from
across the street
welcoming me making me feel my age

older than we would care to acknowledge
or you should admit
the sophistry of it.

Pictures from Brueghel

    I SELF-PORTRAIT
In a red winter hat blue
eyes smiling
just the head and shoulders

crowded on the canvas
arms folded one
big ear the right showing

the face slightly tilted
a heavy wool coat
with broad buttons

gathered at the neck reveals
a bulbous nose
but the eyes red-rimmed

from overuse he must have
driven them hard
but the delicate wrists

show him to have been a
man unused to
manual labor unshaved his

blond beard half trimmed
no time for any-
thing but his painting

II LANDSCAPE WITH THE FALL OF ICARUS
According to Brueghel
when Icarus fell
it was spring

a farmer was ploughing
his field
the whole pageantry

of the year was
awake tingling
near

the edge of the sea
concerned
with itself

sweating in the sun
that melted
the wings' wax

unsignificantly
off the coast
there was

a splash quite unnoticed
this was
Icarus drowning

   III THE HUNTERS IN THE SNOW
The over-all picture is winter
icy mountains
in the background the return

from the hunt it is toward evening
from the left
sturdy hunters lead in

their pack the inn-sign
hanging from a
broken hinge is a stag a crucifix

between his antlers the cold
inn yard is
deserted but for a huge bonfire

that flares wind-driven tended by
women who cluster
about it to the right beyond

the hill is a pattern of skaters
Brueghel the painter
concerned with it all has chosen

a winter-struck bush for his
foreground to
complete the picture . .

    V PEASANT WEDDING
Pour the wine bridegroom
where before you the
bride is enthroned her hair

loose at her temples a head
of ripe wheat is on
the wall beside her the

guests seated at long tables
the bagpipers are ready
there is a hound under

the table the bearded Mayor
is present women in their
starched headgear are

gabbing all but the bride
hands folded in her
lap is awkwardly silent simple

dishes are being served
clabber and what not
from a trestle made of an

unhinged barn door by two
helpers one in a red
coat a spoon in his hatband

      X CHILDREN'S GAMES
I
This is a schoolyard
crowded
with children

of all ages near a village
on a small stream
meandering by

where some boys
are swimming
bare-ass

or climbing a tree in leaf
everything
is motion

elder women are looking
after the small
fry

a play wedding a
christening
nearby one leans

hollering
into
an empty hogshead

Exercise

Maybe it's his wife
the car is an official car
belonging

to a petty police officer
I think
but her get-up

was far from official
for that time
of day

Jersey Lyric

view of winter trees
before
one tree

in the foreground
where
by fresh-fallen

snow
lie 6 woodchunks ready
for the fire

Metric Figure

gotta hold your nose
with the appropriate gesture
smiling

back of
the garbage truck
as the complex

city passes
to the confession
or psychiatric couch or booth

The Gossips

Blocking the sidewalk so
we had to go round
3 carefully coiffured

and perfumed old men
fresh from the barbers
a cartoon by Daumier
reflecting the times were
discussing with a foreign
accent one cupping his
ears not to miss a
syllable the news from
Russia on a view of
the reverse surface of
the moon   .   .

Poem

on getting a card
long delayed
from a poet whom I love
but

with whom I differ
touching
the modern poetic
technique

I was much moved
to hear
from him if
as yet he does not

concede the point
nor is he
indeed conscious of it
no matter

his style
has other outstanding
virtues
which delight me

The High Bridge Above
the Tagus River at Toledo

A young man, alone, on the high bridge over the
      Tagus which was too narrow to allow the sheep
      driven by the lean, enormous dogs whose hind
      legs worked slowly on cogs
to pass easily . . .
      (he didn't speak the language)

Pressed against the parapet either side by the
      crowding sheep, the relentless pressure of the
      dogs communicated itself to him also
above the waters in the gorge below.

They were hounds to him rather than sheep dogs
      because of their size and savage appearance, dog
      tired from the day's work.

The stiff jerking movement of the hind legs, the
      hanging heads at the shepherd's heels, slowly
      followed the excited and crowding sheep.

The whole flock, the shepherd and the dogs, were
      covered with dust as if they had been all day
      long on the road. The pace of the sheep, slow in
      the mass,
governed the man and the dogs. They were
      approaching the city at nightfall, the long
      journey completed.

In old age they walk in the old man's dreams and still
      walk in his dreams, peacefully continuing in his
      verse forever.

Sonnet in Search of an Author

Nude bodies like peeled logs
sometimes give off a sweetest
odor, man and woman

under the trees in full excess
matching the cushion of

aromatic pine-drift fallen
threaded with trailing woodbine
a sonnet might be made of it

Might be made of it! odor of excess
odor of pine needles, odor of
peeled logs, odor of no odor
other than trailing woodbine that

has no odor, odor of a nude woman
sometimes, odor of a man.

The Turtle

(For My Grandson)

Not because of his eyes,
                 the eyes of a bird,
                                 but because he is beaked,
birdlike, to do an injury,
                 has the turtle attracted you.
                                 He is your only pet.
When we are together
                 you talk of nothing else
                                 ascribing all sorts
of murderous motives
                 to his least action.
                                 You ask me
to write a poem,
                 should I have poems to write,
                                 about a turtle.

The turtle lives in the mud
        but is not mud-like,
                you can tell it by his eyes
which are clear.
        When he shall escape
                his present confinement
he will stride about the world
        destroying all
                with his sharp beak.
Whatever opposes him
        in the streets of the city
                shall go down.
Cars will be overturned.
        And upon his back
                shall ride,
to his conquests,
        my Lord,
                you!

You shall be master!
        In the beginning
                there was a great tortoise
who supported the world.
        Upon him
                all ultimately
rests.
        Without him
                nothing will stand.
He is all wise

and can outrun the hare.
                        In the night
his eyes carry him
                to unknown places.
                        He is your friend.

To My Friend Ezra Pound

or he were a Jew or a
Welshman
I hope they do give you the Nobel Prize
it would serve you right
                —in perpetuity
with such a name

If I were a dog
I'd sit down on a cold pavement
in the rain
to wait for a friend (and so would you)
if it so pleased me
even if it were January or Zukofsky

Your English
is not specific enough
As a writer of poems
you show yourself to be inept not to say
usurious

Heel & Toe to the End

Gagarin says, in ecstasy,
he could have
gone on forever

he floated
ate and sang
and when he emerged from that

one hundred eight minutes off
the surface of
the earth he was smiling

Then he returned
to take his place
among the rest of us

from all that division and
subtraction a measure
toe and heel

heel and toe he felt
as if he had
been dancing

Stormy

what name could
better
explode from

a sleeping pup
but this
leaping

to his feet
Stormy!
Stormy! Stormy!

BIOGRAPHICAL NOTE

William Carlos Williams was born on September 17, 1883, in Rutherford, New Jersey. His English father had been raised in the West Indies, and his mother was born in Puerto Rico; Spanish was the dominant language at home. Williams attended public school in Rutherford, lived in Geneva and Paris for two years, and graduated from Horace Mann High School in New York City. He entered the University of Pennsylvania school of dentistry in 1902, then transferred to medical school the following year; while at Penn he began a lifelong friendship with Ezra Pound and met H.D. (Hilda Doolittle) and the painter Charles Demuth. He interned in two New York City hospitals, 1906–09, and published *Poems* (1909) at his own expense. After studying pediatrics at the University of Leipzig for a year, he established a medical practice in Rutherford. He married Florence (Flossie) Herman on December 12, 1912; they had two sons, William Eric and Paul Herman. He published *The Tempers* (1913), and his poem "Postlude" was included in Pound's anthology *Des Imagistes* (1914); Williams' subsequent volumes included *Al Que Quiere!* (1917), *Kora in Hell: Improvisations* (1920), *Sour Grapes* (1921), *The Great American Novel* (1923), *Spring and All* (1923), *A Voyage to Pagany* (1928), and *In the American Grain* (1925). He became acquainted with a circle of poets and artists including Wallace Stevens, Mina Loy, Marcel Duchamp, and Alfred Kreymborg, editor of the journal *Others*, to which Williams was a regular contributor. He joined the Passaic General Hospital as pediatrician in 1924. His *Collected Poems 1921–1931* (1934) was published by the Objectivist Press with an introduction by Wallace Stevens. He published the story collections *The Knife of the Times* (1932) and *Life Along the Passaic River* (1938), the novels *January* (1932) and *White Mule* (1937), and the poetry collections *An Early Martyr and Other Poems* (1935), *Adam & Eve & The City* (1936), *Complete Collected Poems* (1938), *The Broken Span* (1941), and *The Wedge* (1944). His long poem *Paterson* was published in five books between 1946 and 1958. He received the National Book Awards' first Gold Medal for Poetry for *Paterson* in 1950 and shared the 1953 Bollingen Prize with Archibald MacLeish. He suffered the first of a series of strokes in 1952. His last poetry collections were *The Desert Music and Other Poems* (1954), *Journey to Love* (1955), and *Pictures from Brueghel* (1962), for which he was posthumously awarded the Pulitzer Prize. He died on March 4, 1963.

NOTE ON THE TEXTS

The texts of the poems in this volume are taken from the edition published by New Directions in 1986 and 1988: A. Walton Litz and Christopher MacGowan, eds., *The Collected Poems of William Carlos Williams: Volume 1, 1909–1939*, third impression, and Christopher MacGowan, ed., *The Collected Poems of William Carlos Williams: Volume II, 1939–1962*. The list below indicates which of the collections published during Williams' lifetime contained the poems included in the present volume. Books are keyed to the following abbreviations:

T	*The Tempers* (London: Elkin Mathews, 1913)
AQQ	*Al Que Quiere!* (Boston: Four Seas, 1917)
SG	*Sour Grapes* (Boston: Four Seas, 1921)
SA	*Spring and All* (Paris: Contact Editions, 1923)
CP34	*Collected Poems 1921–1931* (New York: Objectivist Press, 1934)
EM	*An Early Martyr and Other Poems* (New York: Alcestis Press, 1935)
AE	*Adam & Eve & the City* (Peru, VT: Alcestis Press, 1936)
CCP	*The Complete Collected Poems* (Norfolk, CT: New Directions, 1938)
B	*The Broken Span* (Norfolk, CT: New Directions, 1941)
W	*The Wedge* (Cummington, MA: Cummington Press, 1944)

C	*The Clouds, Aigeltinger, Russia &c.* (Aurora, NY: Wells College Press and Cummington, MA: Cummington Press, 1948)
CLP	*The Collected Later Poems* (Norfolk, CT: New Directions, 1950)
CLP63	New poems added to CLP for 1963 revised edition
CEP	*The Collected Earlier Poems* (Norfolk, CT: New Directions, 1951)
DM	*The Desert Music* (New York: Random House, 1954)
JL	*Journey to Love* (New York: Random House, 1955)
PB	*Pictures from Brueghel* (New York: New Directions, 1962)

Peace on Earth. T, CEP, CCP.

Con Brio. T, CEP, CCP.

Aux Imagistes. Not collected by Williams. Published in *The Egoist*, December 1914.

Metric Figure ("Veils of clarity"). Not collected by Williams. Published in *Others*, February 1916.

Stillness. Not collected by Williams. Published in *Others: An Anthology of the New Verse* (1916).

The Young Housewife. CCP, SP, CEP.

Pastoral ("When I was younger"). AQQ, CCP, CEP.

Metric Figure ("There is a bird"). AQQ, CCP, CEP.

Apology. AQQ, CCP, CEP.

Pastoral ("The little sparrows"). AQQ, CCP, SP, CEP.

El Hombre. AQQ, CCP, SP, CEP.

Danse Russe. AQQ, CCP, SP, CEP.

Smell! AQQ, CCP, SP, CEP.

Spring Strains. AQQ, CCP, SP, CEP.

January Morning. AQQ, CCP, SP, CEP.

To a Solitary Disciple. AQQ, CCP, CEP.

Dedication for a Plot of Ground. AQQ, CCP, SP. CEP.

Love Song. AQQ, CCP, SP, CEP.

Le Médecin Malgré Lui. CCP, CEP.

A Coronal. CP34, CCP, SP, CEP.

To Mark Anthony in Heaven. CP34, CCP, SP, CEP.

Portrait of a Lady. CP34, CCP, SP, CEP.

Willow Poem. SG, CCP, CEP.

Approach of Winter. SG, CCP, CEP.

January. SG, CCP, CEP.

To Waken an Old Lady. SG, CCP, SP, CEP.

Complaint. SG, CCP, SP, CEP.

Thursday. SG, CCP, CEP.

Play. SG, CCP, CEP.

Complete Destruction. SG, CCP, CEP.

Queen-Anne's-Lace. SG, CCP, SP, CEP.

Waiting. SG, CCP, SP, CEP.

Arrival. SG, CCP, SP, CEP.

Blueflags. SG, CCP, CEP.

The Widow's Lament in Springtime. SG, CCP, SP, CEP.

The Lonely Street. SG, CCP, SP, CEP.

The Great Figure. SG, CCP, CEP.

"By the road to the contagious hospital." SA, CCP. Under the title "Spring and All": SP, CEP.

"The farmer in deep thought." SA, CCP. Under the title "The Farmer": EM, CEP.

"The Easter stars are shining": SA, CCP. Under the title "Flight to the City": CP34, CEP.

"The rose is obsolete": SA. CCP. Under the title "The Rose": SP, CEP.

"In passing with my mind": SA, CCP. Under the title "Young Love": CP. Under the title "Young Romance": EM.

"Of death": SA, CCP. Under the title "Death the Barber": CEP.

"O tongue": SA, CCP. Under the title "To an Old Jaundiced Woman": CEP.

"The pure products of America": SA, CCP. Under the title "To Elsie": CP34, SP, CEP.

"so much depends": SA, CCP. Under the title "The Red Wheelbarrow": CP34, SP, CEP.

"Somebody dies every four minutes": SA, CCP. Under the title "Rapid Transit": CP34, CEP.

"The crowd at the ball game": SA, CCP. Under the title "At the Ball Game": CP34, SP, CEP.

My Luv. Not collected by Williams. Published (without a title) in *Manuscripts*, February 1922.

The Bull. CP34, CCP, SP, CEP.

Fish. CEP.

The Drunkard. CEP.

The Dead Baby. EM, CCP, CEP.

Winter. CP34, CCP, CEP.

On Gay Wallpaper. CP34, CCP, SP, CEP.

The Lily. CP34, CCP, SP, CEP.

9/30 "There are no perfect waves—": CCP, SP, CEP.

10/21 "In the dead weeds a rubbish heap": CCP, CEP.

10/28 "in this strong light": CCP, SP, CEP.

10/29 "The justice of poverty": CP34, CCP, CEP.

11/1 "The moon, the dried weeds": CP34, CCP, CEP.

11/20 "Even idiots grow old": CCP, CEP.

The Moon—. Not collected by Williams. Published in *Blues*, Spring 1930.

Child and Vegetables. Not collected by Williams. Published in *This Quarter*, April–June 1930.

The Trees. CP34, CCP, SP, CEP.

The Wind Increases. EM, CCP, SP, CEP.

The Sea-Elephant. CP34, CCP, SP, CEP.

Death. CP34, CCP, SP, CEP.

The Botticellian Trees. CP34, CCP, SP, CEP.

Poem ("As the cat"): CP34, CCP, SP, CEP.

Nantucket. CP34, CCP, SP, CEP.

This Is Just To Say. CP34, CCP, SP, CEP.

An Early Martyr. EM, CCP, CEP.

Flowers by the Sea. EM, CCP, SP, CEP.

To a Poor Old Woman. EM, CCP, SP, CEP.

Proletarian Portrait. EM, CCP, SP, CEP.

The Raper from Passenack. EM, CCP, CEP.

Genesis. EM.

The Yachts. EM, CCP, SP, CEP.

Fine Work with Pitch and Copper. AE, CCP, SP, CEP.

St. Francis Einstein of the Daffodils. AE, CCP, SP, CEP.

Advent of Today. CCP, CEP.

Classic Scene. CCP, CEP.

Autumn. CCP, CEP.

The Term. CCP, SP, CEP.

The Poor. CCP, SP.

Between Walls. CCP, SP, CEP.

Middle. CCP, CEP.

These. CCP, SP, CEP.

The Last Words of My English Grandmother. B, SP, CEP.

River Rhyme. Not collected by Williams. Published in *Poetry*, November 1940.

The End of the Parade. B, W, CLP.

River Rhyme II. Not collected by Williams. Published in John C. Thirlwall, "The Lost Poems of William Carlos Williams or the Past Recaptured," *New Directions* 16 (1957).

Election Day. Not published in Williams' lifetime.

Passaic, N.J. Not collected by Williams. Published in *The Harvard Advocate*, April 1942.

Gothic Candor. Not collected by Williams. Published in *American Prefaces*, Summer 1943.

A Sort of a Song. W, SP, CLP.

Paterson: The Falls. W, SP, CLP.

The Dance. W, SP, CLP.

Burning the Christmas Greens. W, SP, CLP.

Raleigh Was Right. B, W, SP, CLP.

To Ford Madox Ford in Heaven. W, SP, CLP.

A Woman in Front of a Bank. C, CLP.

When Structure Fails Rhyme Attempts to Come to the Rescue. C, CLP.

Threnody. CLP63.

East Coocoo. CLP63.

The Woodpecker. CLP.

Passer Domesticus. CEP.

The Descent. DM, PB.

To a Dog Injured in the Street. DM, PB.

The Yellow Flower. DM, PB.

The Artist. DM, PB.

Theocritus: Idyl I. DM, PB.

A Negro Woman. JL, PB.

To a Man Dying on His Feet. JL, PB.

The Pink Locust. JL, PB.

from Asphodel, That Greeny Flower: Book I. DM (as "Work in Progress"), JL, PB; Coda: JL, PB.

Sappho. Not collected by Williams. Published in *Poems in Folio* (1957), and also in *Evergreen Review* (Fall 1957), and *Spectrum* (Fall 1957).

Greeting for Old Age. Not published during Williams' lifetime.

from Pictures from Brueghel. PB.

Exercise. PB.

Jersey Lyric. PB.

Metric Figure ("gotta hold your nose"). PB.

The Gossips. PB.

Poem. PB.
The High Bridge Above the Tagus River at Toledo. PB.
Sonnet in Search of an Author. PB.
The Turtle. PB.
To My Friend Ezra Pound. PB.
Heel & Toe to the End. PB.
Stormy. Not published during Williams' lifetime.

NOTES

3.1   Aux Imagistes]   To the Imagists.

13.26   *Half Moon*]   Ship in which Henry Hudson sailed up the Hudson River to the vicinity of present-day Albany, New York, in 1609.

16.4   Park Avenue]   In Rutherford, New Jersey.

18.5   Emily Dickinson Wellcome]   Williams' grandmother; born in England in 1837, she died in 1920.

20.9   Le Médecin Malgré Lui]   "The doctor in spite of himself," the title of a 1666 play by Molière.

44.19   Elsie]   Retarded nursemaid, hired from the state orphanage, who worked for Williams and his family.

55.6   *huldra*]   Long-tailed siren in Scandinavian legend.

55.9   *nekke*]   Water sprite.

88.1   St. Francis . . . Daffodils]   When this poem was included in *Modern Poetry* (1951), Kimon Friar and John Malcolm Brinnin, eds., it was accompanied by Williams' note: "It is always spring time for the mind when great discoveries are made. Is not Einstein, at the same time, saintly in the purity of his scientific imagining? And if a saint it seems to me that the thorough logic which St. Francis saw as sparrows or donkeys, equally to be loved with whatever other living aspect of the world, would apply equally to Einstein's arrival in the United States a number of years ago to celebrate the event in the season's shapes and colors of that moment."

Williams had published another poem with this title (and commemorating the same event) in 1921.

98.4 The Last Words . . . Grandmother] An earlier version of this poem was published in 1924.

106.1 Burning . . . Greens] When this poem was included in *Modern Poetry* (1951), Kimon Friar and John Malcolm Brinnin, eds., it was accompanied by Williams' note: "An occurrence in our home. Certainly no one can escape the conclusion that this poem envisages a rebirth of the 'state' perhaps but certainly of the mind following the destruction of the shibboleths of tradition which often comfort it."

109.1 Raleigh Was Right] Cf. Walter Raleigh, "The Nymph's Reply to the Shepherd," a rejoinder to Christopher Marlowe's "The Passionate Shepherd to His Love."

119.1–3 A drowsy numbness . . . I had drunk.] Cf. John Keats, "Ode to a Nightingale" (1819): "My heart aches, and a drowsy numbness pains / My sense, as though of hemlock I had drunk . . . "

119.5 René Char] French poet (1907–88) who fought with the Resistance during World War II.

124.2 Mr. T.] Identified by Williams as Harry Taylor, a retired professional dancer who assisted at the nursing home where Williams' mother lived.

149.23 Kung] Confucius.

150.16–18 "Sweet Thames . . . my song,"] Cf. Edmund Spenser, "Prothalamion" (1596).

151.22 Sappho] This is a translation of Sappho's Fragment 71. When it was published in *Poems in Folio* (1957), Williams included this note: "I'm 73 years old. I've gone on living as I could as a doctor and writing poetry on the side. I practiced to get money to live as I please, and what pleases me is to write poetry.

"I don't speak English, but the American idiom. I don't know how to write anything else, and I refuse to learn. I'm writing and planning something all the time. I have nothing to do—a retired doctor who can't use his right hand anymore. But my coco (my head, you know) goes on spinning and maybe occasionally I work it pretty hard. It goes on day and night. All my life I've never stopped thinking. I think all writing is a disease. You can't stop it.

"I have worked with two or three friends in making the translation for I am no Greek scholar but have been veritably shocked by the official British translations of a marvelous poem by one of the greatest poets of all time. How their ears can have sanctioned the enormities that they produced is more than I can understand. American scholars must have been scared off by the difficulties of the job not to have done better. Their prosy versions were little better—to my taste. It may be that I also have failed but all I can say is that as far as I have been able to do I have been as accurate as the meaning of the words permitted—always with a sense of our own American idiom to instruct me."

165.18   Zukofsky] Poet Louis Zukofsky (1904–78), a friend of Williams from the mid-1920s on. Williams dedicated *The Wedge* (1944) to Zukofsky.

166.2   Gagarin] Yuri Gagarin (1934–68), Soviet cosmonaut who in 1961 was the first person to travel in space.

167.1   Stormy] When this poem was published in *Poetry* shortly after Williams' death, it was accompanied by the note: "Stormy is the name of the Williamses' Shetland sheep-dog."

INDEX OF TITLES
AND FIRST LINES

AMERICAN POETS PROJECT